796.3232

P648w

DETROIT PUBLIC LIBRARY

3 5674 02425470 9

W9-DAU-602

Winning Basketball

DETROIT PUBLIC LIBRARY

CONELY BRANCH LIBRARY
4600 MARTIN AVENUE
DETROIT, MICHIGAN 48210
898-2426

DATE DUE

JAN 3 1 1996

MAR 0 2 1996

AUG 03

AUG 04

JUL 07

APR 08

BC-3

JAN. 1996

Winning Basketball

TECHNIQUES AND DRILLS FOR PLAYING BETTER BASKETBALL

Ralph L. Pim, Ed.D.
Foreword by Dan Majerle

CB
CONTEMPORARY BOOKS
CHICAGO

Library of Congress Cataloging-in-Publication Data

Pim, Ralph L.
   Winning basketball : techniques and drills for playing
better basketball / Ralph L. Pim.
        p.   cm.
   Includes index.
   ISBN 0-8092-3553-6 (paper)
   1. Basketball—Offense   2. Basketball—Training.   I. Title.
GV889.P49   1994
796.323'2—dc20   94-30923
                                                        CIP

Copyright © 1994 by Ralph Pim
All rights reserved
Published by Contemporary Books, Inc.
Two Prudential Plaza, Chicago, Illinois 60601-6790
Manufactured in the United States of America
International Standard Book Number: 0-8092-3553-6
10   9   8   7   6   5   4   3   2   1

Contents

Foreword by Dan Majerle

My love for the game of basketball began many years ago. My father taught the fundamentals of the game to my brothers and me when we were youngsters. We spent the majority of our free time practicing basketball. Our neighbors got used to hearing the sound of a bouncing ball coming from our backyard basketball court. It was a way of life at the Majerle house.

My parents encouraged us to participate in all sports. Their lives revolved around our practice sessions and games. Sports were the main topics of conversation at our dinner table. In high school I played football, basketball, and baseball. At Central Michigan University I also played baseball and basketball. My younger brother, Jeff, who was a teammate of mine there, later played professional basketball in the Continental Basketball Association and in New Zealand. Steve, my older brother, was a standout on several nationally ranked teams at Hope College.

I learned from my parents that it takes hard work to be successful. Everyone wants to be good, but very few people are willing to make the necessary sacrifices. Any success that I have attained has been the result of my desire and determination. I realized I had limitations, but I made a commitment to become the best player possible. To accomplish this I knew I had to work hard every day. I spent hours and hours developing my shot. Many times I had to shovel the snow off the court before I could practice. I skipped rope and did toe-raises to improve my quickness and jumping ability. I did push-ups in front of the TV to increase my upper-body strength. I did ballhandling drills in the house to improve my dribbling skills. I was constantly searching for ways to improve.

As a young player I always tried to play against better competition. Fortunately, one of my high school coaches, Tom Kozelko, played three seasons for the Washington Bullets in the NBA. He taught me a lot about the game, and we would always play one-on-one after practice. That was a real learning experience—my basketball skills developed much faster because of Tom.

My fondest memories are of the championship seasons that I have experienced on the high school, college, and professional levels. Championship teams have good chemistry. Their players are unselfish and know how to complement each other's strengths. As a high school senior, for example, I could not have averaged over 37 points per game without the cooperation of my teammates. We were a close-knit group and everyone played his necessary role in order to be successful. In the NBA I have established a reputation as a three-point shooter. In 1994 I set the all-time NBA record for the most three-point field goals in a single season. The majority of my baskets are the result of good passes from my teammates. I never judge my game solely on the number of points I score. I always try to help our team win in ways that don't necessarily show up on a statistic sheet.

I have had to overcome several injuries during my playing career. I was unable to play my first year at Central Michigan because of a back injury. It was very difficult sitting out an entire season. To make matters worse, I missed half of the following season due to injuries. With the Suns, I have had to overcome mononucleosis, arthroscopic knee surgery, a separated shoulder, and removal of a benign synovial cyst. It took mental toughness, perseverance, and hard work to battle these problems.

I'm flattered when people refer to me as the NBA's version of Pete Rose. I always admired Rose for his hustle. I pride myself in giving the maximum effort every time I play. I'm not the type of person who can go out on the court and coast. I never want to be outworked in anything I do. When I was at Central Michigan, we were required to do a mile run prior to the start of the season. I won the race every year because I trained hard and refused to settle for anything less than first place. My pride would not allow me to lose.

Dan Majerle

At the 1988 Olympic trials, I knew my intensity and aggressiveness were the key factors in making the team. I worked hard every second I was on the court. I never allowed the coaches to see me resting. I wanted to earn their respect and show them that I would do whatever was necessary to be successful. I made the squad and led the team in scoring and minutes played. It was a great experience, but I was disappointed we did not win the gold medal. I look forward to representing the United States on Dream Team II.

In the game of basketball you are always faced with new challenges. Being selected the 14th pick of the NBA draft was an honor, but I knew that I had to raise the level of my game. On draft day many Phoenix fans booed when my name was announced as their first-round choice. I was determined to show them that the Suns had not made a mistake. I was confident that I could become a key performer in the NBA. I worked hard to earn the respect of everyone in the Suns organization. Winning the 1993 NBA Western Conference Championship and representing Phoenix in the 1992 and 1993 All-Star Games were very exciting and rewarding experiences for me.

Through the years many rewards have come to me because of basketball. I have worked very hard and made many sacrifices, but I also have been very fortunate. I am able to make my living doing something I truly love. I consider myself very lucky, and I hope I can put back into the game a small portion of what it has given me.

My friendship with Coach Pim began when I was a junior in high school, and he recruited me to attend Central Michigan University. Coach Pim is an outstanding teacher and coach. He truly understands the game and has the ability to break down the fundamentals for easy comprehension and fast learning. This book is perfect for players who want to improve their game. I hope you enjoy *Winning Basketball*—I know it will help you on your quest for basketball success.

Offensive player	◯
Offensive player with the ball	⊗
Defensive player	✗
Pass (and direction)	– – – – – ▶
Dribble	∿∿∿▶
Screen or pick	───────┤
Player movement	──────▶
"V" Cut	ⅤＶ

KEY TO DIAGRAMS

1
Basketball Philosophy

1   The Winning Edge

Many people do not truly understand the meaning of success. They believe basketball success means making the NBA All-Star Team or being an All-American. Nothing could be further from the truth. Success is not measured by national recognition or financial rewards. True success begins with focusing all of your resources on becoming the best player possible. It comes from the satisfaction of knowing that you have given your best effort. Successful players strive to realize their potential.

PREREQUISITES FOR ATHLETIC SUCCESS

Only a small difference separates the physical abilities of good athletes and great athletes. Great athletes use their mental attitude to gain an edge over their competition. The following mental factors are instrumental in determining basketball success:

Confidence

Your self-confidence controls your success. The more you believe in yourself the better you will become. Self-confidence is dependent upon your **self-image** and your **self-expectancy**.

Your self-image is how you think about yourself. It sets boundaries for your accomplishments by defining what you can and can't do. If you think you're not a good basketball player, you won't be. Winners see themselves as successful long before success actually happens because they have a positive self-image. There is no factor more important in life than the way you think about yourself.

Confidence is
the key to an
athlete's success.

Your self-expectancy is what you think will happen in the future. Successful athletes expect good things to happen. They believe that if they work hard they will be rewarded.

The fastest way to build confidence is through hard work and dedication. The more you practice, the greater will be your self-confidence.

Concentration

Concentration is the ability to stay focused on a particular task. It is essential to achieve your best performance. As your ability to concentrate improves, so will your performance.

An athlete's concentration can be affected by external as well as internal disturbances. External disturbances include crowd noise, music, poor officiating, or unsportsmanlike behavior from the opposition. Internal disturbances are thoughts such as "My legs are tired," "I really blew that play," or "I hope I don't shoot an air ball." Successful athletes are able to eliminate any type of interference and keep their minds focused on the job at hand.

Athletes must concentrate and stay focused on their goals.

Perseverance

Basketball success does not happen overnight. Every player encounters many setbacks throughout the course of a season or a career. Successful athletes have the ability to rebound quickly from mistakes and disappointments. They do not worry about things they cannot control. Once the play or game is over, they move on to the next challenge. They have the abiliity to stay positive and maintain their motivation during difficult times.

The true test of a team or a group of players is how they handle adversity. Winners are survivors—they find a way to achieve success.

Relaxation

Most players and coaches do not realize that poor performance during competition is often the result of overarousal. Many coaches get their players too psyched before a big game. As a result, the players become overanxious, and their performance is tense.

Athletes experience anxiety for other reasons. Some try too hard—they are under the false impression that if they try harder, they will play better. Others worry too much about making a mistake. Their worry causes their muscles to tighten, thus inhibiting their performance.

Peak performance is dependent upon smooth and natural movements. Successful athletes learn how to relax their minds and their bodies so their movements are spontaneous and natural.

CHARACTERISTICS OF SUCCESSFUL ATHLETES

Success in basketball is not necessarily dependent upon size or athletic ability. Successful players exhibit the following characteristics:

Positive Attitude

A successful basketball player is optimistic and focuses on the positive rather than dwelling on the negative. Find something positive in every situation and never allow problems to destroy your attitude.

Some players have difficulty staying positive after a poor performance. Remember—basketball is a game of mistakes. Focus on the things you did right and don't dwell on your mistakes.

Players should listen closely to their coaches and learn how to accept constructive criticism without looking for an alibi.

Successful players have a burning desire to reach the top.

Desire

Successful athletes have a burning desire to succeed. They want to become the very best they can be. They are always searching for ways to improve.

Never be satisfied with your playing ability. There is always room for improvement in the game of basketball. One way to improve is to listen closely to your coach. Learn how to accept constructive criticism without looking for an alibi.

Determination

Successful performers find a way to succeed regardless of the obstacles that are placed in their path. This driving force is called determination.

Determined athletes exhibit a tremendous work ethic. They understand there are no short cuts to success—it takes hours and hours of hard work.

Many people do not reach their goals because they do not extend themselves. Never settle for anything less than the best you can be. Always work hard and give the maximum effort. Be the first player on the floor at practice and the last one to leave. Establish a reputation for giving 100 percent every time you pick up a ball.

Determination is what drives players to succeed.

Mental Toughness

The achievement of success is based on the power of the mind. The right attitude is the key to everything in this world. Success is there for everybody, but it requires extreme mental toughness.

Outstanding players do not let distractions or setbacks affect their performance. They stay focused and concentrate on the job that must be done. You must find a way to perform up to your potential, even under adverse conditions.

Enthusiasm

Successful athletes enjoy playing and demonstrating their love for the game. Basketball should be fun. Don't be afraid to show your enthusiasm as you play.

Players should show their love for the game
with enthusiasm and a positive attitude.

Unselfishness

Basketball is a team game. Everyone must work together and get along in order to be successful. This does not mean that you have to be best friends with all of your teammates. But it does mean that you have to be willing to make sacrifices and fit within the structure of the team by playing a specific role. It is your responsibility to learn, accept, and play the role that will best help your team.

It is amazing what a team can accomplish if no one cares who gets the credit. Selfishness and dissension will destroy a team.

Everyone must work together for a team to be successful.

STEPS TO SUCCESS

Becoming a successful athlete does not happen by accident. It takes planning, hard work, and continual assessment of your progress. The following steps will help in your drive for success:

Decide What You Want to Accomplish

Successful athletes have a clear understanding of what they want to accomplish. They establish short-range and long-range goals to help attain the desired end result. They make a total commitment to reach their goals. Setting goals not only improves performance but also increases self-confidence and motivation. Set goals that are high enough to present a challenge but still are within reach.

Take Action

Successful performers take complete responsibility for reaching their goals. They realize that they control their success. To become an outstanding

It takes hours of hard work both on and off the court to become an outstanding player.

player is their responsibility—no one can do it for them.

It is important to have a plan for every training session. Determine a definite practice time as well as a list of drills that must be done. The quality of your practice time is much more valuable than the quantity.

Constantly Evaluate Your Progress

Continual evaluation is necessary to enhance your performance. Goals must be evaluated to determine if they are set either too high or too low.

Redirect Your Plan of Action If Necessary

Successful athletes redirect their plan of action when they are not making progress. Their goals may have been set too high, or their work strategies may need to be changed. Whatever the case, establish a new course of action when necessary.

SELF-ASSESSMENT INVENTORY

To assist in your development as a basketball player, answer the following questions as honestly and objectively as possible.

After recording your responses, ask your coach to do the same thing. Compare the results and work on those areas that need improvement.

Key
5—Almost always
4—Most of the time
3—Sometimes
2—Seldom
1—Almost never

1. What are your goals for the upcoming season?

_____

_____

_____

2. Are you totally committed to reaching your goals?

     1   2   3   4   5

3. Do you exhibit confidence in your playing ability?

     1   2   3   4   5

4. Are you receptive to constructive criticism from your coach?

1   2   3   4   5

5. Do you demonstrate an intense desire to succeed?

1   2   3   4   5

6. Do you encourage and compliment your teammates?

1   2   3   4   5

7. Do you fully extend yourself during practice?

1   2   3   4   5

8. Do distractions affect your performance?

1   2   3   4   5

9. Do you work hard during the off-season to improve?

1   2   3   4   5

10. Are you able to bounce back easily from setbacks or disappointments?

1   2   3   4   5

2
Offensive Fundamentals

2 Shooting

Shooting is the most important fundamental in the game of basketball. Regardless of how well a team does everything else, if it cannot score points it will not be successful.

The Phoenix Suns, for example, succeeded because of their high-scoring offense. The Suns led the NBA in scoring in 1993 and 1994. Opponents could not stop the powerful inside play of Charles Barkley or the three-point shooting of the Suns' perimeter players. As a result, Phoenix compiled the best record in the league and won the Western Conference Championship in 1993.

Shooting also is the most enjoyable and most practiced fundamental in the game of basketball. Everyone wants to become a better shooter. It is exciting to score points. All players dream of making the game-winning basket or being the leading scorer on their team. But remember—shooting is a skill. To become a good shooter, you must be willing to spend hours and hours practicing the correct fundamentals.

DEVELOP A SHOOTER'S MENTALITY

Good shooters develop the ability to score under pressure. Look at Game Six of the 1993 NBA Finals, when John Paxson hit the game-winning three-point shot to win the championship. Every player on the floor knew the ball was going in the basket as soon as Paxson caught the pass. Players such as John Paxson are said to have a shooter's mentality—they have that special ability to make clutch shots.

Shooting is the most enjoyable and most practiced fundamental in the game of basketball.

To develop a shooter's mentality, you must have **concentration** and **confidence**.

Concentration

- Focus on the basket with every shot attempt.
- Ignore all distractions.

Confidence

- Believe in yourself as a shooter.
- Remember the shots you made—not your misses.
- Picture yourself as a successful shooter.
- Confidence develops from hours and hours of perfect practice.

Remember the formula for shooting success:

CONCENTRATION + CONFIDENCE = BASKET

Good shooters exhibit concentration and confidence.

The shooter must focus on the basket with every shot attempt.

PERFECT PRACTICE MAKES PERFECT

The old saying "practice makes perfect" can be improved by the addition of a single word: "*perfect* practice makes perfect." This definitely is the case in shooting. Players must practice the correct fundamentals in order to become outstanding shooters.

STEP ONE: AN EAGERNESS TO LEARN

The first step to becoming a great shooter is an eagerness to learn. You must be willing to listen and take constructive criticism from your coach. It takes tremendous desire and dedication to become an outstanding shooter.

Coaches must motivate and provide feedback to players to assist in their development as shooters. All coaches should understand the fundamentals of shooting and be able to teach the correct shooting techniques.

DEVELOP A SHOOTING STYLE BASED ON SOUND FUNDAMENTALS

The foundation of a great shooting style always consists of solid fundamentals. Great shooters vary somewhat in their styles, but their shooting techniques are fundamentally sound. Understanding and implementing the correct shooting techniques is essential for success in this game.

FUNDAMENTALS OF PERIMETER SHOOTING

There are many important fundamentals involved in shooting a basketball. The following list provides key facts in becoming an outstanding shooter:

Balance
- The shot starts from the floor up.
- Feet are shoulder-width apart with the foot of the shooting hand slightly ahead.

All shots must be balanced.

A shooter's shoulders face squarely toward the basket and his toes are pointed at the target.

- Toes are pointed at the basket.
- Shoulders are square to the basket.
- Head is kept straight with no lateral or backward movement.

Grip

- The shooting hand is centered on the ball.
- The fingers of the shooting hand are spread comfortably, with the ball touching the whole hand except for the palm.
- The forefinger and the thumb of the shooting hand form the shape of the letter "V."
- The nonshooting hand, called the balance hand, is kept on the side of the ball.

The shooting hand is centered on the ball, with the ball touching the whole hand except for the palm.

The fingers of the shooting hand are spread comfortably.

The balance hand is on the side of the ball.

Wrist

- Lock the wrist and cock it back.
- As a check, you should see wrinkles on the back of your wrist if the ball is cocked properly. (Cocking the ball in the shooting pocket is called "loading the gun.")

Elbow

- Keep the elbow *under* the ball, not out to the side.
- The elbow is pointed at the basket.
- The elbow is closer to the target than the wrist—this will ensure that the ball is cocked properly and helps avoid "pushing" the ball to the basket.

The elbow is kept under the ball during the shot attempt.

The wrist is cocked slightly over or slightly in front of the forehead. During the wrist cock, the elbow is closer to the basket than the wrist.

Shooting Alignment
- The shooting foot, elbow, wrist, and hand are all on the same plane with the basket.
- The ball is brought up past the face.

Sighting the Basket
- Concentrate on the rim before, during, and after the shot attempt.
- Do not lift the head to watch the flight of the ball.

The head is kept still during the shot and is positioned directly over the body.

The ball is lifted as the fingers are thrust up and forward through the ball.

The ball should be released near the top of the jump.

Release of the Ball

- The legs initiate the shot and the toes are used as springboards.
- The fingers are thrust up and forward through the ball.
- The wrist snaps, releasing the ball off the thumb, index, and middle fingers.
- To get the correct movement of the arm and wrist during the shot,

The ball rolls off the fingers as the wrist snaps.

The ball should be released at a 60-degree angle to ensure the proper trajectory.

visualize shooting over a seven-foot defender or shooting out of the top of a telephone booth without hitting the side walls.

- The wrist movement and finger thrust create the proper backspin necessary for a soft shot.
- Release the ball near the top of the jump.
- The best angle of release for shooting is 60 degrees.

Follow-Through

- The follow-through is necessary to insure the proper arc and ball rotation.
- There is complete elbow extension and wrist flexion during the follow-through.
- To get the correct follow-through, visualize reaching into a cookie jar or putting your hand into the basket.

The fingers should wave good-bye to the ball.

There is complete elbow extension and wrist flexion during the follow-through.

The shooter should hold the follow-through and stay balanced as he returns to the floor.

TEACHING PROGRESSION FOR PERIMETER SHOOTING

Load the Gun

Face the basket with the feet shoulder-width apart. Cock the ball in the shooting pocket. Hold this position and check the position of the feet, elbow, wrist, and hands.

Shoot for the Stars

Lay down on your back with the ball in the shooting pocket. Using the proper grip, cock the wrist, and extend the shooting arm into the air. Release the ball with the correct follow-through. Shoot the ball to yourself and repeat the procedure.

Shoot Off the Board

Combine all shooting techniques and shoot the ball off the backboard. The purpose of this drill is to practice the correct fundamentals without worrying if the ball is going into the basket.

Nothing But Net

Start in front of the basket and shoot the ball, attempting to hit only net. After making several shots, move back one step. Repeat this procedure until you have reached the free-throw line.

SHOOTING CHECKPOINTS

After learning the key shooting fundamentals, use these check-points to establish sound shooting habits:

1. Feet are shoulder-width apart.
2. Toes are pointed at the basket.
3. The shooting hand is centered on the ball.
4. The wrist is cocked back.
5. The elbow is in front of the wrist and is pointed at the basket.
6. The elbow is kept under the ball.

7. The fingers are thrust up and forward through the ball (wave good-bye to the ball).
8. Follow through with complete elbow extension and wrist flexion (hold the follow-through).

COACHES' EVALUATION SHEET FOR SHOOTING

Coaches must provide feedback to their players in regard to shooting technique. One way to do this is a written evaluation. The following is an example of an evaluation sheet:

SHOOTING EVALUATION SHEET

Player: _____ Date: _____

Shooting Fundamentals	Excellent	Good	Fair	Poor
Feet shoulder-width apart	____	____	____	____
Shooting foot slightly ahead	____	____	____	____
Toes pointed at the basket	____	____	____	____
Shooting hand centered on the ball	____	____	____	____
Balance hand on the side of ball	____	____	____	____
Ball cocked in the shooting pocket	____	____	____	____
Elbow in front of wrists	____	____	____	____
Elbow pointed at the basket	____	____	____	____
Elbow under the ball	____	____	____	____
Fingers thrust up and forward	____	____	____	____

	Excellent	Good	Fair	Poor
60-degree arc on shot	___	___	___	___
Elbow extension on follow-through	___	___	___	___
Wrist flexion on follow-through	___	___	___	___
Backspin on the ball	___	___	___	___
Head is kept still	___	___	___	___

Mental Attitude for Shooting

	Excellent	Good	Fair	Poor
Readiness to learn	___	___	___	___
Concentration	___	___	___	___
Confidence	___	___	___	___
Knows shooting range	___	___	___	___
Knows when open	___	___	___	___

Preparation for Shot

	Excellent	Good	Fair	Poor
Hands ready	___	___	___	___
Knees bent	___	___	___	___
Footwork for shot off the dribble	___	___	___	___
Footwork for shot from a pass	___	___	___	___

Comments:_____

_____

_____

MAKE ADJUSTMENTS FOR YOUNGER PLAYERS

It is important for coaches to teach players to understand what a good shot looks like and feels like. For the very young player this is impossible with a regulation-size ball and a 10-foot basket. Make adjustments for these beginning players by using a smaller ball and lowering the basket to either 8 or 9 feet. Remember that developing sound shooting mechanics is the first step to becoming an outstanding scorer.

FUNDAMENTALS OF THE LAYUP

- Keep your head up and concentrate on the target.
- Dribble with the hand away from the defense.
- Bring the nondribbling hand to the ball so that the ball is kept away from the defender.
- Take the ball up with two hands for protection.

Concentrate on the basket and take the ball up with two hands when shooting the layup.

- Jump off the foot opposite the shooting hand and drive the other leg and knee up and toward the basket (high-jump toward the basket rather than long-jump).
- Release the ball at the top of the jump.
- Use the backboard when driving to the basket from the wing.
- Shoot the ball softly off the board (hit the top corner of the backboard square).
- When driving down the middle of the floor or from the corner, shoot the ball over the top of the rim using the underhand layup.

Jump off the foot opposite the shooting hand and drive the other leg and knee up and toward the basket.

Lay the ball over the top of the rim when driving down the middle of the floor.

TEACHING PROGRESSION FOR LAYUP SHOOTING

Step and Shoot

Position yourself two steps away from the basket at a 45-degree angle from the backboard. Take one step with the foot opposite the shooting hand. Drive the other leg and knee up and toward the basket. Shoot the ball softly off the top corner of the backboard square.

Dribble and Shoot

Start three steps away from the basket. Take the first step with the same foot as the shooting hand. Dribble once, jump off the inside foot, and drive the other leg and knee up and toward the basket.

TYPES OF LAYUPS

Overhand Layup

- Use when approaching the basket at high speed.
- The shooting hand is in front and under the ball.
- The fingers point upward.
- The ball is released by a slight flick of the wrist, fingers, and elbows.

The shooting hand is positioned on the back of the ball in the overhand layup shot.

Underhand Layup

- Use when approaching the basket at high speed.
- The shooting hand is in front and under the ball.
- The fingers point upward.
- The ball is released by a slight flick of the wrist, fingers, and elbows.

The shooting hand is in front and under the ball
in the underhand layup shot.

Power Layup

- Use when closely defended.
- Come to a jump stop with the shoulders parallel to the baseline.
- The toes point toward the baseline.
- Take the ball up with two hands for protection.
- Jump off both feet and use your body for protection.
- Shoot using the hand away from the defensive player.
- Use the backboard.

Jump off both feet and keep the shoulders parallel to the baseline when taking the power layup shot.

Reverse Layup

- Use when you are forced under the basket and come out the other side for a shot; also, after securing a rebound or loose ball under the basket.
- It is a difficult shot to block because you use the rim for protection.
- Your back faces the basket at the time of the shot.
- The head is tilted backward and the eyes are focused on the basket.
- The ball is taken upward with both hands.
- The palm of the shooting hand faces the basket and the ball is shot in front and above the head.

The reverse layup shot is difficult to block because the shooter uses the rim for protection.

The dunk shot is one of the most exciting plays in basketball.

Dunk Shot

- Use when your jump takes you above the rim.
- It is one of the most exciting plays in basketball.

THE FREE THROW

Most close games are decided at the free-throw line. In 1993 the Phoenix Suns won 11 of 17 games that were decided by three points or less. A big reason for the Suns' success in close games was their excellent free-throw shooting. Phoenix converted over 75 percent of its free throws and led the NBA in the number of free throws made.

Points scored from free throws make up a large percentage of the total point production. In both the NBA and college basketball, approximately 20 to 25 percent of a team's points are scored from the free-throw line.

The free-throw line is the perfect place to help your team and boost your scoring average. In the course of a basketball season most players get a lot of free-throw attempts: NBA star David Robinson, of the San Antonio Spurs, attempted over 900 free throws during the 1994 season.

Surprisingly, however, most players do not spend enough time practicing their free throws. This no doubt explains the decline in free-throw accuracy at the college level. In 1993 the free-throw shooting percentage in college basketball was the lowest in over 30 years.

Through hours of practicing the correct shooting fundamentals, you can improve your free-throw percentage. A perfect example of this is Karl Malone, of the Utah Jazz: Malone wasn't a good free-throw shooter when he entered the NBA—in fact, he made only 48 percent of his free throws during his rookie season. But as a result of hard work and dedication, he now shoots over 70 percent from the charity stripe.

IMPROVING YOUR FREE-THROW SHOOTING

The best way to improve your free-throw shooting is to establish a routine that you follow on every attempt. Routines vary from player to player, but the end result is a consistent technique. This will assure you that your free-throw attempt will be the same regardless of the situation or score.

The national average for free-throw shooting in college is 68 percent; the NBA average is 73 percent. A realistic goal for most high school and college players is 70 percent. A good model is Mark Price, of the Cleveland Cavaliers. Price shoots almost 90 percent from the foul line and has an excellent routine and a picture-perfect shot.

ⓘFREE-THROW ROUTINE

The following routine is highly recommended for free-throw shooting:

1. Place your feet in the correct shooting position.
   - Shooting foot—directly in line with the middle of the rim, turned at a 10-degree angle
   - Nonshooting foot—several inches behind and 12–14 inches apart from the shooting foot, turned at a 45-degree angle

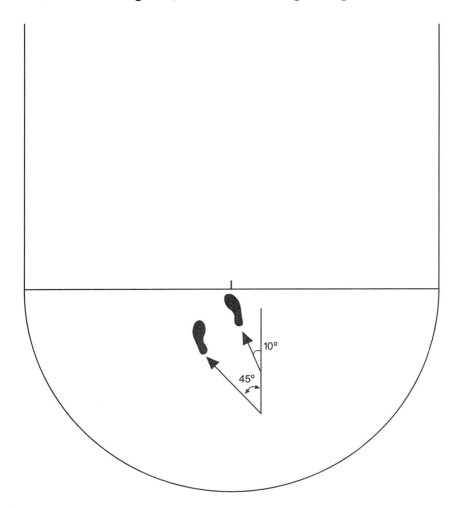

Position of the feet when shooting a free throw (right-handed shooter)

2. Bend the knees slightly.
3. Bounce the ball a set number of times.
4. Establish the correct hand position on the ball.
5. Cock the ball in the shooting pocket.
6. Concentrate on the basket.
7. Initiate the shot with the legs.
8. Extend the shooting arm in a fluid motion.
9. Follow through.

Establish a free-throw routine based on sound shooting fundamentals.

THE THREE-POINT SHOT

Over the past 10 years nothing has changed basketball as much as three-point shooting. A three-pointer is psychologically the most powerful play in the game—it demoralizes the defense and is the quickest way to build momentum. The three-point shot—or "home run," as it is called in the NBA—has brought tremendous excitement to basketball.

Today, players are shooting three-pointers more than ever before. From 1987 to 1993, the number of three-point attempts in college basketball increased 79 percent—approximately one of every four shots is taken from the three-point range. Three-point baskets accounted for 23 percent of the scoring in college basketball in 1994. As a result, three-point shooting has become a key component in the offensive and defensive strategies of all coaches.

In 1993 the Suns set an NBA record for the number of three-point field goals made. Phoenix finished with 398 treys, almost doubling the total from the previous year. The addition of Charles Barkley opened three-point shooting opportunities for Danny Ainge and Dan Majerle. Majerle tied for the league lead in three-point field goals made and also set several records during the NBA playoffs for three-point shooting. Danny Ainge finished eighth in three-point shooting accuracy. In fact, Ainge was the only player in the league to take more than half of his total shot attempts from outside the three-point arc.

The three-point shot has placed an even higher premium on shooting. The "pure shooter" has become a catalyst for basketball in the 1990s. Every team has a place for the player who can hit the three-point shot.

GUIDELINES FOR THREE-POINT SHOOTING

Becoming a successful three-point shooter takes time and practice. The following suggestions will help you become a better three-point scorer:

Know Where the Three-Point Line Is at All Times

- Never take a shot when stepping on the line.
- Spot up in the three-point area in your early offense.
- Relocate to a three-point shooting area after feeding the post.

One of every four shots in college basketball is a three-point attempt.

Be Ready to Shoot the Three-Point Shot
- Get your hands up, ready to receive the pass.
- Bend your knees and get your legs ready to initiate the shot.

On the one-count stop, the feet hit
the floor at the same time.

When shooting off the dribble, a player
plants the inside foot and pivots toward
the basket.

Always Be Moving Toward the Basket on the Shot

- Never take the shot falling away from the basket.
- Use your legs to increase your shooting range.
- Shoot the ball on the way up.

Hold the Follow-Through

- Do not throw the ball at the basket (cock the wrist and use the same shooting technique prescribed for a two-point field goal).
- Your hand and arm motion is the same on all perimeter shots.

FOOTWORK PRIOR TO SHOOTING

Many coaches and players underestimate the importance of footwork prior to shooting. Footwork is the key to getting the shot off quickly and maintaining balance. Two basic types of footwork that can be used from a pass or a dribble are the one-count stop and the plant-and-pivot.

One-Count Stop

The one-count stop is accomplished by jumping slightly from the basket-side foot and landing in the shooting position with a staggered stance. Both feet hit the floor at the same time. The one-count stop is recommended because it can be done quickly.

When shooting off the dribble, coordinate the last dribble with the last step on your basket-side foot. This should be a hard dribble in order to quickly place the ball in the "shooting pocket"—in front of your chest near your dominant shoulder.

Plant-and-Pivot

The plant-and-pivot is executed by landing on your basket-side foot and pivoting so your toes are facing the basket. The other foot lands soon after and is placed in the proper shooting position.

When shooting off the dribble, coordinate the last dribble with the plant step. Lower the inside shoulder as the body is turned into the shooting position.

SHOT SELECTION

Successful teams generally shoot a higher field-goal percentage than their opponents. For this to happen, each player must understand proper shot selection. Knowing when not to shoot is just as important as knowing when

A successful shooter uses good judgment and takes high-percentage shots.

to shoot. For example, the Chicago Bulls won back-to-back NBA titles in 1991 and 1992 shooting over 50 percent from the floor because each player had a clear understanding of when to shoot.

One of the more difficult tasks of a coach is teaching shot discipline. Coaches can assist players in learning their shooting range by keeping accurate statistics and charting shooting drills.

GUIDELINES FOR SHOT SELECTION

The following guidelines will help you pick your shot:

Be Within Your Shooting Range
For two-point field-goal attempts your shooting range is that area in which you can make at least 50 percent of your shots; for three, at least 33 percent of your shots.

No Defender Has a Hand in Your Face
Shooters must be well balanced and get a good look at the basket. Avoid shooting when closely defended. A hand in your face significantly lowers your shooting percentage.

No Teammate Has a Better Shot
You must see the floor and look for open teammates. If a teammate has a better shooting opportunity, pass the ball to that individual.

The Rebounding Areas Are Covered
Avoid perimeter shots when your rebounders are not close to the basket. It is important that your teammates are in the proper rebounding positions in case you miss your shot.

The Score and Time Indicate a Need for This Shot
What may be a good shot at one point in the game may be a bad shot at another point. Shot selection is always decided by the score and the amount of time left to play.

3 Passing

Passing is the foundation for teamwork and scoring. Next to shooting it is the most important offensive fundamental. Defensive players have difficulty reacting to good passes. Consequently, good passing teams end up with high-percentage shots.

There was a time in basketball when passing was in danger of becoming a lost art—good passers were a rarity. But in the 1980s players such as Magic Johnson and Larry Bird brought a new dimension to the game with their outstanding and creative passing.

Regardless of your size, you need to be able to handle the ball and make good passes. Many of the centers in the NBA are excellent passers. Brad Daugherty, a seven-footer, is adept at finding the open man and making exceptional passes.

Passing is the foundation for teamwork and scoring.

LEARN TO "SEE" THE FLOOR

The first step to becoming a good passer is learning how to "see" the floor. John Stockton, of the Utah Jazz, is one of the best at correctly analyzing the situation on each possession before deciding where to pass the ball.

It is the passer's responsibility to determine if the receiver is open. To pass successfully, you need to key on your potential receivers and their defenders.

A good passer sees the floor and passes to teammates when they are open.

See Your Receivers

- Recognize their floor position and readiness for a pass.
- Anticipate any cutting action or movement.

See the Defense

- See the floor position of the defensive player guarding the pass receiver.
- Recognize the amount of pressure your defender is applying.

The passer should key on the receiver and the defenders.

CREATE OPEN PASSING LANES

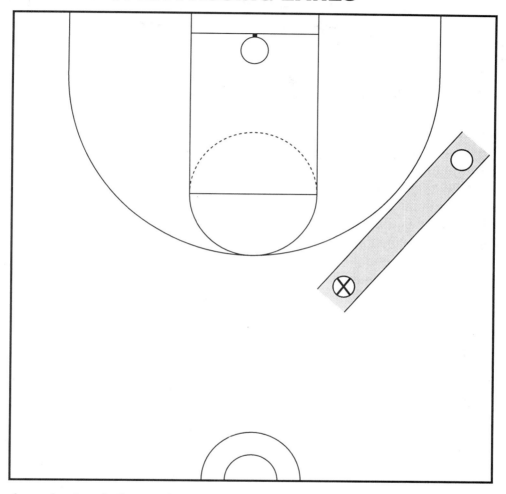

A passing lane is the area between two offensive players
where a pass could be made.

Good passers create open passing lanes. A passing lane is the area between
two offensive players where a pass could be made. Your objective as a
passer is to create a passing lane that is free of defenders. Two ways to open
passing lanes are by dribbling and faking.

A ball handler can dribble to open a passing lane when his defender
plays loosely. A sagging defensive player has too much time to react to the

Two ways to create passing lanes
are by dribbling and by faking.

pass after it has been thrown. Dribbling toward the defender will freeze that player and allow a pass to be completed.

Dribbling also may be necessary to create a passing lane when the defender plays the ball handler tightly. A quick dribble to either side will get the defender out of the passing lane and establish a better passing angle.

Faking is another technique used to open a passing lane. An effective fake changes the defender's hand position or floor position. Moving the defender creates an opening for a pass to a teammate.

ELEMENTS OF A GOOD PASS

Whereas excellent shooters make only 50 percent of their shots, good passers should be almost 100 percent effective. Here are the basic elements of good passing and key teaching points:

Accuracy
- Pass the ball to a spot where your teammate can do something with it.
- Aim for the shooting pocket.
- Always throw the ball to the side away from the defender.

Timing
- The pass must be delivered when the receiver is open.
- A late pass is a poor pass.
- The quickest and safest passes are direct passes, not bounce passes.

Quickness
- Pass the ball quickly, before the defender has time to react.
- Do not wind up when you pass the ball.
- Keep two hands on the ball until you release the pass.
- Always pass through or past a defender.
- Pass the ball ahead to an open player whenever possible.

Deception
- Use fakes to open passing lanes.
- Fake in one direction and pass in the opposite direction.

The passer should throw the ball through
or past a defender.

The ball should be passed ahead to an
open teammate whenever possible.

CATCHING PASSES

Passing and catching go together—you cannot have a successful pass without a successful reception. Very often players and coaches do not spend time practicing the fundamentals of catching. Many turnovers are caused by a lack of concentration on the part of the receiver. Here are some key points to remember when catching a pass:

Give the Passer a Target
- Keep your hands up.
- Show the passer where you want the ball thrown.

The receiver should always keep his hands up and give a target to the passer.

Meet Each Pass

- Move toward the ball until contact is made (cut toward the pass or take a step and reach for the ball).
- Grip the ball in a thumbs-up position.
- Move the ball from the triple-threat position (see Chapter 5) to the center of your chest and keep it close to your body.
- Bend the body forward and step toward the receiver.
- Release the ball by extending the elbows as the thumbs turn down and the palms rotate outward.
- Push the thumbs through the ball to produce backspin.

The receiver should move toward the ball and meet each pass.

Watch the Ball into Your Hands

- Concentrate on the flight of the ball.
- Catch the ball with your eyes.
- Do not begin your next move before actually catching the ball.

Catch the Ball with Two Hands

- Do not try to catch the ball with one hand.
- Relax your fingers and thumbs prior to catching the ball.
- As you make contact with the ball, allow your hands and arms to give toward your body.

Assume the Triple-Threat Position

- Always put the ball in the triple-threat position (see Chapter 5).

The receiver must concentrate on the flight of the ball and catch the ball with two hands.

After catching a pass, a player should put the ball in the triple-threat position.

TYPES OF PASSES

Chest Pass

The chest pass is the most effective and efficient pass for ball movement. It is used to get the ball to a teammate quickly when there is no defender in the passing lane.

The chest pass is the most effective and efficient pass for ball movement.

Bounce Pass

The bounce pass is often used at the end of a fast break or when passing to a player in the post or to a player making a back-door cut. A shot fake or high-pass fake usually precedes a bounce pass. Remember—the bounce pass is the slowest of all passes.

On the bounce pass, the ball should bounce at a point about two-thirds of the distance between the passer and the receiver.

- The grip is the same as that for the chest pass.
- Bend the body forward and step toward the receiver.
- Release the ball by extending the elbows as the thumbs turn down and palms rotate outward.
- Push the thumbs through the ball to produce backspin.
- The ball should bounce at a point about two-thirds of the distance between the passer and the receiver.
- The receiver should catch the ball waist-high.

Overhead Pass

The overhead pass is used very effectively against a zone defense because it allows the ball handler to pass from one side of the court to the other. It also can be used as an outlet pass to initiate a fast break or to feed the post.

The overhead pass is released with a quick snap of the wrist and fingers.

- Grip the ball with fingers pointed upward and thumbs on the back of the ball pointing inward.
- Bring the ball to a point directly over your head (do not wind up and bring the ball behind your head).
- Step forward with the pass.
- Release the ball with a quick snap of the wrist and fingers.
- Keep your elbows slightly flexed during the throw.
- The receiver should catch the ball at about chin level.

Baseball Pass

The baseball pass is used as a long pass to a cutter breaking toward the basket. It also is used to inbound the ball quickly after a score. This is a difficult pass to control, and accuracy is very important.

- Your body should be parallel to the sidelines.
- The passing hand is behind the ball while the other hand is in front and slightly under the ball.
- Plant the rear foot and step with the front foot toward the receiver.
- Keep two hands on the ball as long as possible.
- Throw the ball from behind the ear with the force provided by a quick wrist snap and arm thrust.
- Follow through with full pronation and extension of the arm.

Push Pass

The push pass is used to pass through or past a defender who is guarding closely. It can be either a direct or a bounce pass and is often preceded with a vertical fake (example: fake high, pass low).

The push pass is a one-handed pass. The force is provided by a quick wrist snap.

- Start the ball in the triple-threat position (see Chapter 5) with one hand behind and the other hand on the side of the ball.
- The force of the pass is provided by a quick wrist snap.
- Release the ball past the defender.

Behind-the-Back Pass

The behind-the-back pass is often used in a fast-break situation when two offensive players are attacking one defender. It is a very effective pass as long as it is used in the right situation. It can be either a direct or a bounce pass.

- Cup the ball in your throwing hand.
- Swing your arm in a circular path around the body and behind the back.
- The force of the pass is provided by a whip of the arm and by finger flexion on the release.

4
Dribbling

For beginning players, dribbling is probably the most misused and over-used fundamental. Young players often make the mistake of dribbling the ball once immediately after catching a pass, thus wasting their dribble. Beginning players also tend to overdribble and not gain any advantage over their defenders. Players must learn to always dribble with a purpose.

REASONS TO DRIBBLE

Good basketball players use dribbling to create scoring opportunities. Before beginning their dribble, they assess the situation by looking at their basket, seeing both the offensive and defensive players. They will then use the dribble to:

- Penetrate toward the basket
- Advance the ball upcourt
- Improve a passing angle
- Get out of trouble

GUIDELINES FOR DRIBBLING

Regardless of your size or what position you play, you must be able to dribble the ball effectively. The following points will help you become a better dribbler:

The primary objective of dribbling is to create a scoring opportunity.

Dribble with a Purpose
- Never put the ball on the floor unless you have a reason to dribble.
- The primary objective of dribbling is to create a scoring opportunity.

Keep Your Head Up
- See the entire floor.
- Focus your attention on the basket.
- Dribble without watching the ball.

Dribble with the Hand Farthest from the Defender

- Always protect the ball.
- Keep your body between the ball and your defender.

Never Pick Up the Dribble Without a Pass or a Shot

- Once you start your dribble, keep it alive until you pass or shoot.
- Picking up your dribble allows defenders to pressure you because they no longer have to worry about dribble penetration.

Do Not Dribble into Trouble

- Use your dribble wisely.
- Do not dribble between two defenders or into the corners of the court.
- Be alert for traps.

The dribbler should keep his head up and dribble with the hand farthest from the defender.

FUNDAMENTALS OF DRIBBLING

- The dribbling hand should be cupped and the fingers spread comfortably.
- The dribble is a push-pull motion of the arm, wrist, and fingers.
- Initiate the dribble by elbow extension and flexion of the fingers and wrist.
- Meet the bouncing ball with your fingers, with your wrist absorbing the upward force.
- Control the ball with the fingers and the pads of the hand, not the palm.
- Keep the nondribbling arm up for protection.

The hand is cupped, the fingers are spread comfortably, and the ball is controlled by the fingers and the pads of the dribbling hand.

CONTROLLING THE BALL

The placement of your hand on the ball is the key to controlling your dribble. Practice dribbling with your hand on each of these areas of the ball: directly on top, in front, behind, on the right side, and on the left side. This develops excellent ball control and prepares you for a variety of dribble moves that you can use to outmaneuver defenders.

TYPES OF DRIBBLE MOVES

You should become skilled in the use of each of the following types of dribbles:

Control Dribble

Use the control dribble when you are closely guarded. Protect the ball by keeping your body between the ball and the defensive player.

- Dribble the ball at knee level or lower.
- Use a staggered stance with the ball-side foot back.
- Advance the ball with a step-and-slide movement.
- Keep the free arm up for protection.
- Keep the elbow of the dribbling arm close to the body.

The control dribble is used when the dribbler is closely guarded.

The speed dribble is used in the open court to advance the ball quickly.

Speed Dribble

Use the speed dribble in the open court to advance the ball quickly.

- Keep your body nearly erect, leaning slightly forward.
- Extend your dribbling arm fully, pushing the ball out in front of your body.
- Dribble the ball near waist level or higher to attain maximum speed.

Change-of-Pace Dribble

Use the change-of-pace dribble to penetrate past a defender. Its purpose is to make the defensive player believe that the ball handler is slowing down. When the defender relaxes, the dribbler drives toward the basket. The offensive player continues to dribble with the same hand and in the same direction as before the hesitation.

- When slowing down, plant your lead foot, straighten up slightly, and throw your head up to relax the defender.
- Accelerate quickly by pushing off the ball of your lead foot.
- Use a low dribble to go past the defender.

The change-of-pace dribble is used to penetrate past a defender.

Crossover Dribble

Use the crossover dribble to make a sharp directional change. It can be especially effective when you are being overplayed. The advantage of the crossover dribble is that you never lose visual contact with the basket and your teammates. The disadvantage is that you may expose the ball to your defender if you are being guarded too closely.

- When the foot on the dribbling side contacts the floor, push off hard toward the opposite foot.
- Slide the dribbling hand to the outside and top of the ball.
- Force the ball across your body on a diagonal path with a flick of your wrist and fingers.
- Reach down with the receiving hand to get the ball on a short hop at the same time as you take a step with the foot on that side.
- Your receiving hand should be cupped and should give slightly when it receives the ball.
- Complete the move with a long crossover step by the foot on the original side of the dribble.

Spin Dribble

The spin dribble is also called the reverse dribble. Use it to change direction when you are closely guarded and the crossover dribble is too dangerous to attempt. The advantage of the spin dribble is that your body is always between the ball and the defender. The disadvantage is that you momentarily lose visual contact with the basket and your teammates.

- When initiating the spin dribble with a right-hand dribble, stop with the left foot forward and pivot on the ball of the left foot.
- At the same time, "pull" the ball close to your body with the right hand until you complete the pivot and make the first step with your right foot.
- After completing the rear turn, switch the ball to the opposite hand.
- Turn your head quickly in order to see the floor.

Behind-the-Back Dribble

The behind-the-back dribble is another way to change direction. This technique is safer than the crossover dribble and quicker than the spin dribble. Another advantage is that you always maintain visual contact with the basket.

- When you initiate the behind-the-back dribble with the right hand, your weight should be on your right foot as you put your right hand on the outside of the ball.
- Push the ball with a quick flick of the wrist and fingers and a whipping motion of the lower arm.
- As you move your left foot forward, bounce the ball behind your back and into your left hand, continuing the dribble.

Between-the-Legs Dribble

Use the between-the-legs dribble to force a defender off balance so you can penetrate toward the basket. It is an effective dribble when you are being overplayed.

- You can switch the ball to the opposite hand regardless of which foot is in front.
- Keep the ball low and switch hands.
- Force the ball through your legs with a quick, hard flick of the wrist and fingers and a whipping motion of the lower arm.

The behind-the-back dribble allows the dribbler to always maintain visual contact with the basket.

The between-the-legs dribble is used to force the defender off balance so the dribbler can penetrate toward the basket.

Pull-Back Dribble

Use the pull-back dribble to create spacing whenever the defense tries to double-team or run and jump: you can avoid defensive pressure by moving backward with the dribble.

- Use the control dribble and retreat two steps.
- Push off the front foot and move backward with the rear foot (it is a step-slide movement).
- Keep your head up and see the floor.
- Maintain the dribble until you can make a pass.

The pull-back dribble allows the dribbler to avoid defensive pressure by moving backward with the dribble.

DRIBBLE PENETRATION

Nothing hurts a defense as much as penetration. Whenever the ball gets inside the defense, the end result is normally a high-percentage shot for the offensive team.

The premier point guards in basketball today create scoring opportunities for themselves or their teammates through dribble penetration. The Suns' Kevin Johnson is an explosive player who exhibits blinding speed on his drives to the basket. It is almost impossible to keep him out of the lane; the defense is forced to cover up, which creates open shots for the offense.

Two keys in dribble penetration are getting past your defender and finishing the play.

Dribble penetration really hurts a defense.

Getting Past Your Defender

The first step is finding a way to get past your defender. Kenny Anderson, of the New Jersey Nets, has the ability to squeeze through the smallest of defensive openings. Excellent penetrators like Anderson and Golden State's Tim Hardaway are able to create openings that enable them to drive to the basket. To accomplish this objective, a dribbler must get his defender out of the driving line (an imaginary straight line from the ball handler to the basket).

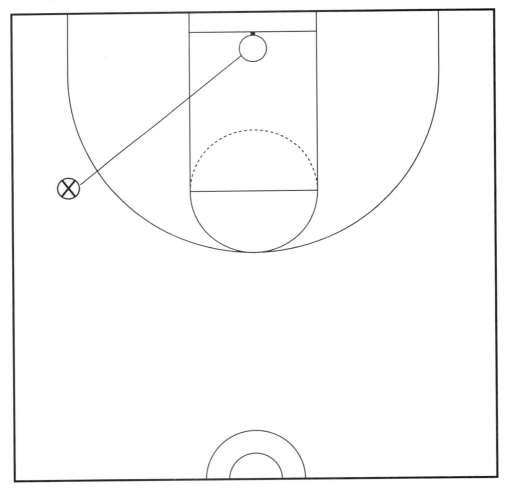

The driving line is an imaginary straight line
from the ball handler to the basket.

One way to open the driving line is by using fakes. When a dribbler is closely guarded, an effective fake will move the defender in a horizontal position away from the driving line. This creates an opening to drive. The faking technique could be a foot fake, such as a jab step, or it could take the form of a head fake or ball fake.

A second way to create an open driving line is by dribbling. Any of the dribbling moves—the crossover, behind-the-back, between-the-legs, or the spin dribble—can be used to get past the defender. Tim Hardaway's crossover dribble is one of the best dribble-penetration moves in the NBA.

When the defender is in a sagging position, the dribbler should gain momentum by dribbling right at the defensive player before executing a dribble move. It is difficult for a stationary defender to contain a penetrating dribbler.

Finishing the Play

Outstanding penetrators must keep their heads ups, see their teammates as well as their defenders, and never dribble into trouble. John Stockton is the best point guard in the NBA at finishing plays after penetrating past his defender. After getting past your defender it is essential to read the situation correctly and finish the play:

- When the driving line is open, penetrate to the basket and score.
- When the defender of a teammate positioned on the perimeter picks you up, pass to the open player for a perimeter jump shot.
- When a post defender steps up to stop you, pass inside to your open teammate.

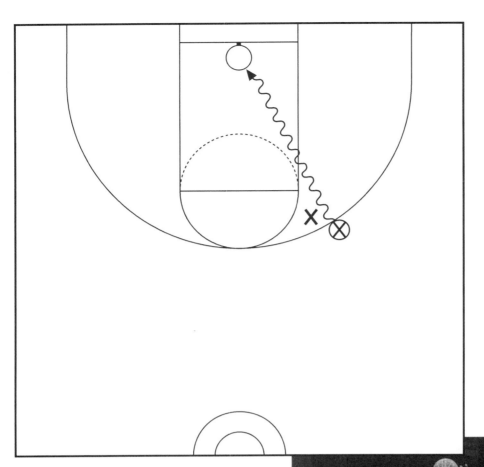

Penetrate and score

When the driving line is open,
the dribbler should penetrate
to the basket and score.

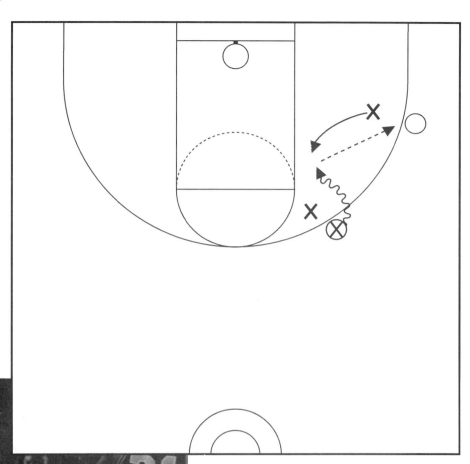

Penetrate and pitch

When a defender from the perimeter picks up the dribbler, he should pass to the open player for a perimeter jump shot.

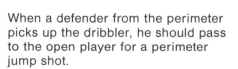

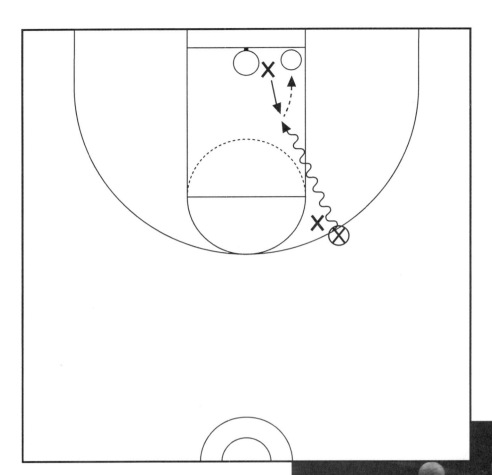

Penetrate and dish

When a post defender steps up
to stop the dribbler, he should
pass inside to the open man.

5   Basic Offensive Skills

Before you can dribble, pass, or shoot effectively, you must move quickly and efficiently. You must be able to accelerate, change directions, and stop abruptly while maintaining your balance. Your ability to move will determine your basketball success.

A player must be able to move quickly and efficiently.

STARTING

Basketball is a game of quickness. During the course of a game, players are continually accelerating from a stationary position. Speed and quickness can be improved through practice of the correct techniques:

- Lower your shoulder and lean your head in the direction you wish to go (the head leads in the weight shift).
- Push hard off your foot (the heel must come in contact with the floor on the push-off).
- Keep leaning when you start forward, and use your arms to accelerate by using a quick, pumping action.

STOPPING

You must be able to stop abruptly and in a balanced position. There are two ways to do this: the *jump stop*, in which you jump off one foot and land on

When stopping, a player should land with knees bent and maintain a wide base of support.

both feet simultaneously in a parallel or staggered stance; and the *stride stop*, also called the one-two stop, in which you land one foot at a time. The advantage of the jump stop is that you can then use either foot as your pivot foot. After the stride stop, you are allowed to use only your rear foot (the one that touches the floor first) as your pivot foot.

Whichever method you use, the following points are important:

- Land with the knees bent.
- Keep the head up and centered over the body.
- Maintain a wide base of support.
- Keep the back fairly straight (do not bend at the waist).

CHANGING DIRECTION

Offensive players must continually change direction in order to get free from their defenders. Here is the best way to change direction when running forward:

1. Slow down.
2. Plant the outside foot and push off that foot.
3. Point and step with the inside foot.

Always maintain a low center of gravity and keep your head centered over your body. Lower your shoulder in the direction you want to go. This type of maneuver is very difficult to defend against.

PIVOTING

Pivoting, the rotation of the body around one foot kept in a stationary position, is the primary technique for initiating almost all changes in direction. It is an essential skill for maintaining balance and quickness. The *front pivot*—stepping forward while turning on the pivot foot—is used when you are not closely guarded by your defender. The *reverse* (or *rear*) *pivot*—stepping backward—is used when you are closely defended.

Remember the following points when pivoting:

- Maintain balance by keeping your feet shoulder-width apart and your knees bent.

- Keep your head up and centered over your body.
- Pivot by lifting up the heel and turning on the ball of your pivot foot.
- Protect the ball by keeping your elbows bent and close to your body.

THE TRIPLE-THREAT POSITION

The triple-threat position is the cornerstone of all offensive basketball fundamentals. It allows you to quickly shoot, pass, or dribble the ball.

After receiving a pass, first look at your basket—many coaches call this movement "catch and face." At the same time, put the ball in front of your chest near your dominant shoulder so you can make a quick offensive play. This area is sometimes called the "shooting pocket."

The classic triple-threat stance is as follows:

- Head is up and centered over the body.
- Eyes are looking at the basket and seeing the floor.
- Body weight is evenly distributed, with the feet shoulder-width apart.
- Knees are bent.
- Shoulders are facing the basket.
- The ball is positioned near the dominant shoulder.

From this position, you should look to do one of the following: shoot, pass inside, pass on the perimeter to continue the offense, or dribble to create an open shot or pass.

READY POSITION

When you do not have the ball, you should be ready to move quickly to receive a pass or help a teammate get open. The following points are helpful when playing without the ball:

- Keep your hands above your waist.
- Keep your eyes on the ball handler and your defender.
- Keep your knees bent.
- Be ready to push off the ball of your foot and move quickly in any direction.

The triple-threat position is the cornerstone for all offensive basketball fundamentals.

After receiving a pass, a player should look at the basket and put the ball in the "shooting pocket."

6   Perimeter Moves

Individual moves are an important part of a team's offense. All players must learn to work together but at the same time use individual moves to create scoring opportunities. You must be capable of beating your defender player in a one-on-one situation.

There are many outstanding one-on-one players in the NBA, but the name that stands above the rest is Michael Jordan. He could take command of any situation on the court. With his athletic skills and his competitive attitude, Jordan was in a league of his own.

The perimeter moves discussed in this chapter are those made by an offensive player when facing the basket.

BASIC PRINCIPLES OF PERIMETER MOVES

Every time you catch the ball on the perimeter, remember to do the following:

- Look at your basket.
- Bring the ball into the triple-threat position.
- Maintain good balance and be a threat to score.
- Use fakes to set up an offensive move.
- All moves must be quick and in a straight line to the basket.
- Read the defense to determine whether to shoot, pass, or drive.

The ball handler must read the defense to determine whether to shoot, pass, or drive.

ATTACKING THE DEFENDER

In order to make the best possible offensive move, you must correctly analyze your defender's floor position and the position of his feet:

- When the defender is in a staggered stance, attack the front foot (the defender's most vulnerable side is the front foot due to the fact that he must make a pivot before he can recover and stop the dribbler).
- When the defender leaves the floor or plays with straight legs, penetrate to the basket.
- When the defender backs up, take the perimeter jump shot.
- When the defender rushes at the ball, drive to the basket.
- When the defender reacts to a fake by moving laterally, penetrate in the opposite direction from the fake.

FAKING

Faking is a technique used to get a defensive player off balance or out of position. To be effective, a fake must look like the real thing. Fakes by a ball handler are designed to open passing lanes, create shots, or open driving lanes to the basket.

An offensive player can use ball fakes, shot fakes, foot fakes, head fakes, or eye fakes to deceive a defender. Many times you need to use a combination of fakes in order to gain an advantage. Generally, players fake in one direction and move in the opposite direction.

- When using foot fakes, always fake into the defensive player as much as possible (do not fake to the side).
- When using shot fakes, do not straighten your legs—when the ball goes up, stay down and keep your knees bent.
- Ball quickness is a key in all pass fakes and shot fakes.
- Use your eyes to look in the same direction as the fake.

On the shot fake, the ball goes up but the knees remain bent.

TYPES OF ONE-ON-ONE MOVES

Every player likes the challenge of playing one-on-one. There is tremendous satisfaction in driving past your opponent and scoring a basket. Practicing the following moves will help you beat your defender in a one-on-one situation.

Direct Drive

The direct drive is used to penetrate past a defender. No fake is necessary with the direct drive because you have a driving lane to the basket. The first step is crucial: it must be a long, quick step with the foot opposite the pivot foot.

- Push off the pivot foot.
- Take a long, quick step with the nonpivot foot.
- Accelerate past your defender by pushing the ball ahead (go somewhere with the dribble).
- Keep your head up.

Jab Step and Drive

A *jab step* is a short, quick step directly at the defender with the nonpivot foot. If the defensive player does not respect the jab step by retreating, dribble penetrate to the basket. As a general rule, anytime you get your foot even with the defender's foot, drive past the player.

- Jab step at the defender (do not bring the foot back to its original position).
- If the defender does not react to the jab step, push off the pivot foot and take a long step past him.

Crossover Step and Drive

The crossover step and drive is used when the defender reacts to a foot fake by moving laterally.

- Make a jab step and then a quick crossover step with the same foot (cross over with a long step past the defender).

- At the same time swing the ball quickly across, keeping it close to the body.
- Keep your inside shoulder between the defender and the ball.
- Keep the pivot foot stationary while you make the jab step and crossover step.
- Push the ball ahead on the floor and drive.

Rocker Step

The rocker step can set up either a drive or a shot from the perimeter. It is used when the defender reacts to a foot fake by moving either forward or backward.

- Make a jab step at the defender to fake a drive to the basket.
- Rock back to the triple-threat position.
- If the defender lunges forward, take a long, quick step and drive.
- If the defender drops off, shoot the jump shot.

As a variation, you can add a shot fake after returning to the triple-threat position. If the defender goes for the fake, dribble drive to the basket.

7   Inside Moves

Every player, regardless of size, must learn how to score inside. Even perimeter players will have opportunities to score inside against defenders similar in size. Perfecting inside moves will help you become a complete offensive scorer.

TEAM SUCCESS DEPENDS ON THE INSIDE GAME

Most coaches build their offense from the inside out. Getting the ball inside helps in the following ways:

- It produces high-percentage shots.
- It increases the chances of being fouled by your opponent.
- It forces the defense to collapse, thus opening up three-point shooting opportunities.

POST-UP STANCE

The first step in becoming an inside scorer is learning how to post up. The correct post-up stance keeps your defender out of the passing lane so that you can receive the pass. You must make contact with your opponent and keep him away from the passing lane. Be prepared for physical contact in the post area.

- Assume a floor position just outside the free-throw lane and above the free-throw block.

Team success is dependent upon establishing an inside game.

When posting up, a player must maintain a wide base and keep his defender out of the passing lane.

The post player should keep his elbows out and give a two-hand target with his fingers spread and pointing upward.

- Maintain a wide base with a low center of gravity.
- Keep your elbows out and parallel to the floor.
- Give a two-hand target with fingers spread and pointing upward.
- Make contact and keep the defender in place ("sit on" the defender's legs).
- Keep the defender on your back (do not allow the defender to step in front).

GETTING OPEN

It is your responsibility to get open so you can receive a pass. There are a number of ways to do this:

- Beat your defender down the floor.
- Make a "V" cut (fake one direction and go the opposite).
- Flash cut to the openings between defenders.
- Step across your defender's front foot in order to establish an open passing lane.
- Execute a reverse pivot to seal your defender from the passing lane (place your foot in between your defender's feet and reverse pivot).

READING THE DEFENSE AND THE BALL HANDLER

Always focus your attention on the floor positions of both the ball handler and your defensive player.

If you are located on the opposite side of the court from the ball, look to flash across the lane into an open area. Your objective is to cut in front of your defender so you have the inside position to receive a pass. When you are on the same side of the court as the ball handler, position yourself on an imaginary line through the ball and the basket. This is called getting "on track" with the passer. It shortens the pass from the post feeder and provides the best passing angle.

Successful inside players always read their defenders in order to create scoring openings. The following guidelines will place you in position to score more effectively:

- If defended on the low side, take the defensive player a step or two lower and post up.
- If defended on the high side, take the defensive player a step or two higher and post up.
- If fronted, move closer to the ball, seal the defender, and look for the lob pass or ball reversal.
- If guarded from behind, establish contact, keep the defender in place, and post up.

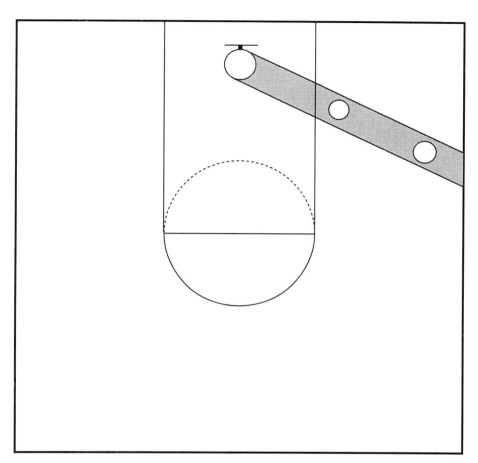

To pass the ball inside, the ball handler and the post man
must get "on track."

THINK ONE PASS AHEAD

Another way to establish open passing lanes is to think one pass ahead.
There are many times when a perimeter player cannot get the ball to you.
Do not give up your post-up position or get discouraged. By maintaining
contact with your defender, you often will create a passing lane from a
different angle.

Imagine that you are posting up on the block and the ball handler is at the wing. Your defender is playing on the low side and prohibits a pass being thrown to you. You must think one pass ahead. Maintain contact and keep the defensive player on the low side. You have established a new passing lane and will be open when the ball is passed out front. Outstanding inside players are always thinking one pass ahead and establishing new passing angles.

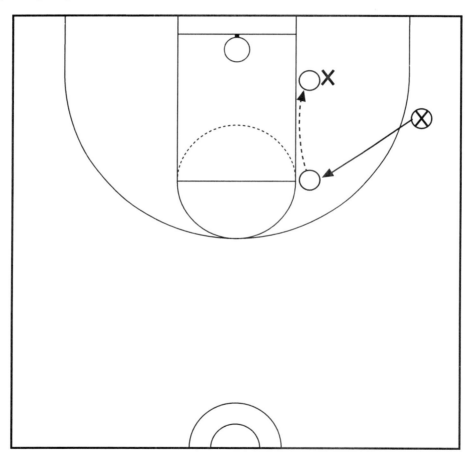

An inside player can create a new passing lane by maintaining contact and keeping the defender on the low side.

CATCHING THE PASS

When receiving the ball from a post feeder, remember the following points:

- Reach for the pass.
- Catch the ball with two hands.
- Bring the ball to your chest immediately.
- Locate and read the defense.

TYPES OF INSIDE MOVES

There are several inside moves that you should perfect. Your choice will depend on the floor position of your defender and how far you are from the basket.

Drop Step

The drop step is used when the defensive player is positioned on the high side. The offensive player can execute the drop step either with or without a dribble.

There isn't a center in the league that can stop Shaquille O'Neal's drop step to the basket. Shaq combines exceptional strength and quickness as he muscles his way for powerful inside moves and dunks.

With the Dribble:
- Pivot using a rear turn on the foot closest to the defender.
- Step toward the basket with the nonpivot foot.
- Seal off the defender with your body.
- Take one quick, low dribble.
- Point the shoulder at the basket.
- Take the ball up with two hands for protection.
- Shoot using the hand farthest from the defender.
- Use the backboard whenever possible.

Without the Dribble.
The only difference is that the post player executes the drop step before catching the pass and does not use the dribble.

When using the drop step, the post player steps toward the basket with his nonpivot foot and seals off the defender.

The offensive player should take the ball up with two hands and shoot using the hand farthest from the defender.

Jump Hook

The jump hook is used when the defender is playing on the low side. This move also can be used with or without a dribble.

Kevin McHale had a picture-perfect jump hook when he played for the Boston Celtics. McHale dominated the low post with his inside moves. His patented jump hook was impossible to block.

With the Dribble:

- Execute a rear-turn pivot with the baseline foot as the pivot foot.
- Use the nonpivot foot to step into the lane (do not step away from the basket—this foot should point toward the sideline).
- Take one quick, low dribble.
- Point your shoulder at the basket.
- When your nonpivot foot hits the floor, swing the pivot foot into the lane (your chest should be facing the sideline).
- Jump off both feet.
- Bring the ball up along the side of your head and release with full arm extension.
- Protect the ball with the nonshooting arm.

Without the Dribble:

- Execute a rear-turn pivot with the baseline foot as the pivot foot.
- Step into the lane with the nonpivot foot—it serves as the take-off foot for the shot.
- Raise your pivot foot and lift your knee high in the air.
- Bring the ball up along the side of your head and release with full arm extension.

Turnaround Jump Shot

The turnaround jump shot can be used when the defender is playing behind or on either side of the post player. The offensive player must create space from the defender in order to get the shot off.

Patrick Ewing has an excellent turnaround jump shot. He is a powerful player inside and is one of the best-shooting centers in the NBA.

- Catch the ball, chin it, and locate the defender.
- Pivot using a front turn on the foot farthest from your defender.
- Keep the ball above your chest during the pivot.
- Square up and take the jump shot.

When shooting the jump hook, release the ball with full arm extension.

Wheel to the Middle

The wheel-to-the-middle move is used when your defender cuts off the drop step. Good inside scorers always have counter moves when defenders stop their initial move.

Dominique Wilkins is one of the most explosive scorers in the league. No matter how the defense tries to stop him, he always finds a way to score. Wilkins performs the wheel-to-the-middle move as quickly as anyone.

- This move is a combination of the drop step and the jump hook.
- Execute a drop step to the basket.
- If your defender slides over to stop the baseline move, pivot to the middle for a jump hook.

Up and Under

The up-and-under move is used to penetrate to the basket after the defensive player reacts to a shot fake. Hakeem Olajuwon, one of the NBA's top centers, uses a quick up-and-under move to score inside.

- Pivot using a front turn and face the basket.
- Execute a shot fake (move the ball up but keep the knees bent).
- If your defender goes up for the fake, step through quickly with the nonpivot foot.
- Bring the ball across your body with speed and quickness.
- Take a long, quick step toward the basket.
- This move can be used with or without a dribble.

8   Moving Without the Ball

Since only one player at a time can handle the ball, theoretically you will be playing without the ball about 80 percent of the time. This statistic clearly illustrates the importance of developing skills without the ball.

Moving without the ball requires you to be adept at starting, stopping, faking, and changing directions. You must have excellent court awareness and vision so that you maintain the proper floor spacing with your teammates.

Many young players do not know how to move efficiently without the ball. They will either run directly toward the ball handler begging for a pass or stand in one place watching the ball handler dribble the ball.

One of the best at moving without the ball in the NBA is Chris Mullin. His superb physical conditioning allows him to stay in perpetual motion. Mullin is a master at freeing himself from his defender and taking his deadly jump shot.

MOVE WITH A PURPOSE

Remember your moves must have a purpose. Your movement should be coordinated with those of your teammates so that you are working as a smooth-functioning unit. You can move to an open area to receive a pass, you can set screens for teammates, or you can clear through to the other side of the court to create more room for the ball handler.

SEE THE BALL AND YOUR DEFENDER
BEFORE CUTTING

See the floor position of both the ball and your defensive player to determine when and where to move. Once you have decided your course of action, push off from the floor hard and move with quickness. Cuts should be sharp and made in a straight line. If you move in an arc, your defender can follow a straight path and beat you to the desired spot.

ALWAYS MAINTAIN FLOOR BALANCE

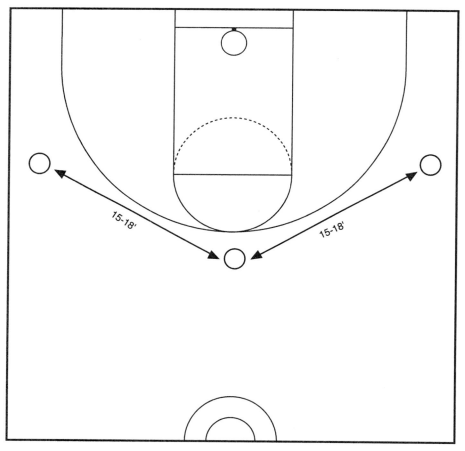

Players positioned on the perimeter must maintain the proper floor balance and be 15–18 feet apart.

One of the most important concepts in team offense is proper spacing. Players should be approximately 15 to 18 feet apart. Be careful not to bring your defender into an area that reduces the effectiveness of one of your teammates.

It is impossible to maintain spacing at all times due to the many screens that are set. It is important, though, to always balance the floor after screening or cutting.

TYPES OF CUTS

You must be able to get open without the use of a screen. To accomplish this, you must become proficient in the following cuts:

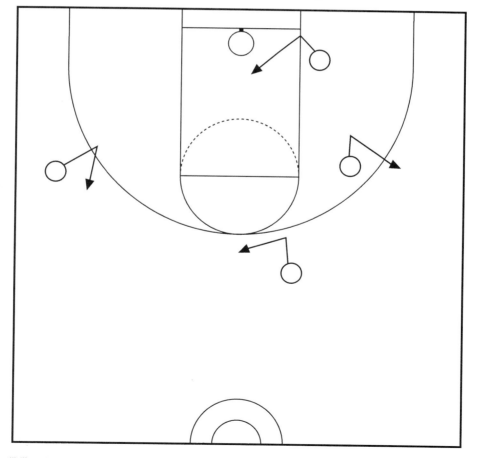

"V" cut

"V" Cut

The "V" cut is a change-of-direction cut that takes the shape of the letter "V." It is designed to move your defender in a direction opposite from your intended cut.

- Move slowly into the "V" cut; then push off hard and make a long stride past your defender.
- Get your hands up and be ready to receive a pass.

Back Cut

The back cut is a cut behind the defensive player and toward the basket. It is often used when your defender is overplaying and denying you the pass.

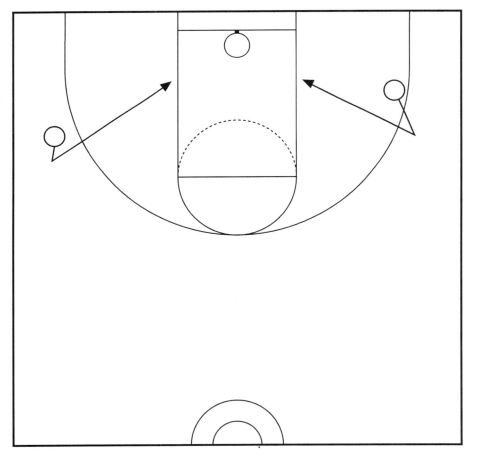

Back cut

The back cut can be executed in one of two ways:

- Pushing off the outside foot and take a long step with the other leg.
- Or pivot on the inside foot and execute a long crossover step toward the basket.
- Never lose sight of the ball.
- Give a hand target for the passer.

"L" Cut

The "L" cut is a change-of-direction cut that takes the shape of the letter "L." Use it when your defender is in the passing lane but is playing very loosely.

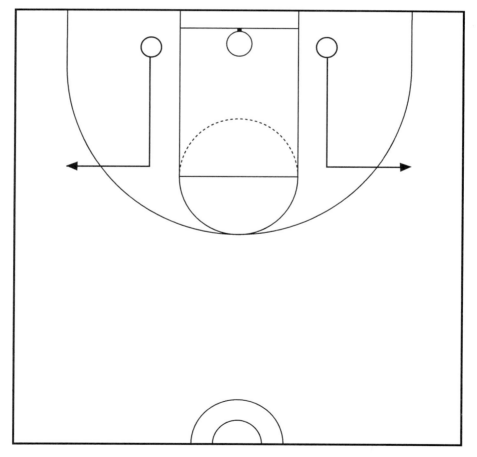

"L" cut

- Move toward your defender; then push off hard and cut to the wing.
- This cut is effective because the offensive player closes the distance, making it difficult for the defender to react to the hard cut.

Inside Cut

An inside cut is used when the offensive player passes the ball to a teammate and cuts to the basket looking for a return pass. This maneuver is sometimes referred to as the "give and go."

- After passing to a teammate, use a "V" cut to set up your defender.

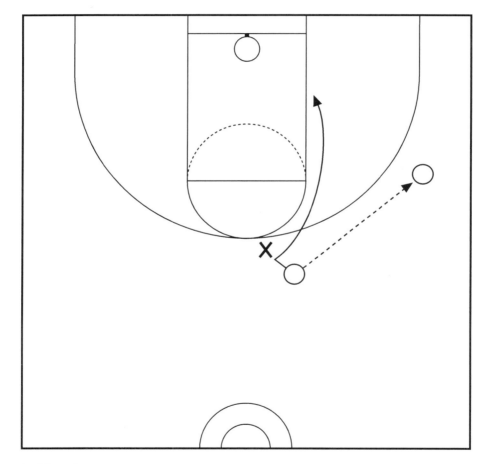

Inside cut

- Make a hard cut in front of your defender, creating an open passing lane.
- Get your hands up and be ready to receive a pass.

Fish-Hook Cut

The fish-hook cut is a change-of-direction cut that is sometimes called a "shallow cut." It is used as a pressure release when you are being over-played and the ball handler is dribbling toward you.

- If you are overplayed, take several steps toward the basket and then move in the opposite direction from the dribbler.

Fish-hook cut

- Make a quick "hook" back toward the ball for a pass from the ball handler.
- This cut is effective because it forces your defender out of the denial position.

Clock-Down Cut

The clock-down cut is a cut toward the baseline by a helpside forward. It is used to create an open passing lane.

- Make a cut toward the baseline when you see a teammate driving to the basket.
- Go as close to the baseline as necessary to create an open passing lane.
- This cut is effective because your defender will normally leave you to help stop the drive to the basket.

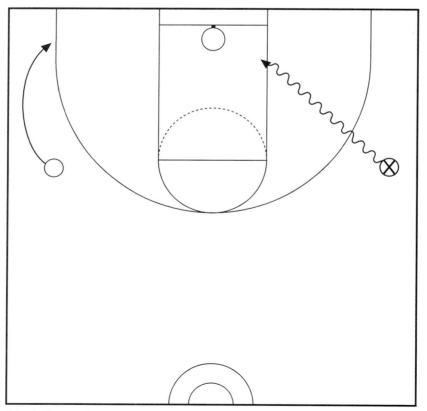

Clock-Down Cut

9   SCREENING

The best way to help a teammate get open is by setting a screen. Effective screening places the defense at a tremendous disadvantage because it is difficult to stay with a cutter coming off a good screen. If the defensive players switch, there is often a mismatch in height or ability. A defensive switch also creates inside positioning for the screener to receive a pass.

SETTING A SCREEN

As a screener, it is your responsibility to get the cutter open for a pass or shot.

Assume a Wide Stance
- Come to a jump stop with the feet shoulder-width apart.
- Place the hands in front of your midsection, both for protection and as a reminder not to overextend, grab, or push the defender.

Establish the Proper Angle
- Set the screen perpendicular to the expected path of the defender.
- Your back should be square to the area where the cutter will receive the pass.
- Set the screen approximately an arm's length away from the defender.

Hold the Screen
- Be firmly set.
- Be ready for contact.

React to the Defender and the Cutter
- When the defender attempts to fight through the screen, the player using the screen is usually open.
- When the defenders switch, the screener will be open.

"Shape Up" After the Screen
- After the screen occurs, turn toward the ball.
- Get your hands up and be ready to receive a pass.

RECEIVING A SCREEN

When a teammate screens for you, it is your responsibility to drive your defender into the screen.

Set Up Your Defender
- Take your defender in a direction opposite that of your intended cut.
- Make a "V" cut prior to using the screen.

Wait for the Screen
- Do not go too early.
- Give the screener time to get set.

Cut Directly Off the Screen
- Drive your defender into the screen.
- Make shoulder contact with the screener as you cut.

Read the Defense
- The type of cut you make is dependent upon the floor position of your defensive player.
- See your defender.

Be Ready for the Pass
- Get your hands up as you come off the screen.

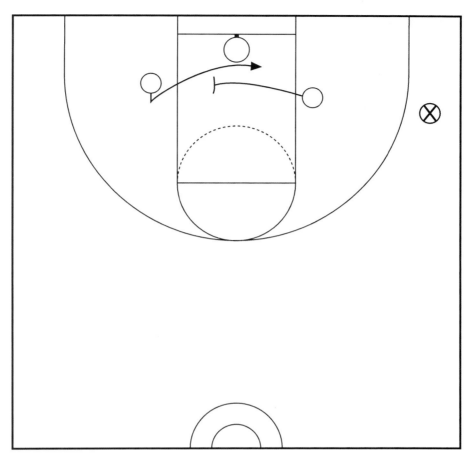

When receiving a screen, wait for the screen to be set and make a "V" cut prior to using the screen.

TYPES OF SCREENS

The floor position of your teammate's defender determines the type of screen that you will set. Learn how and when to use the following screens:

Down Screen

The down screen is used when an offensive player moves toward the baseline to free an offensive cutter on the perimeter.

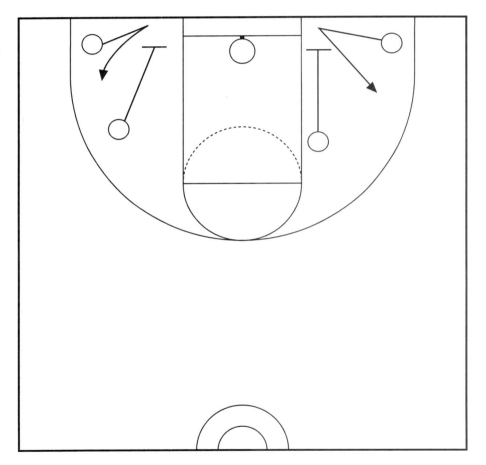

Down screen

Cross Screen

The cross screen is used when an offensive player moves laterally to set a screen for a teammate in the post area.

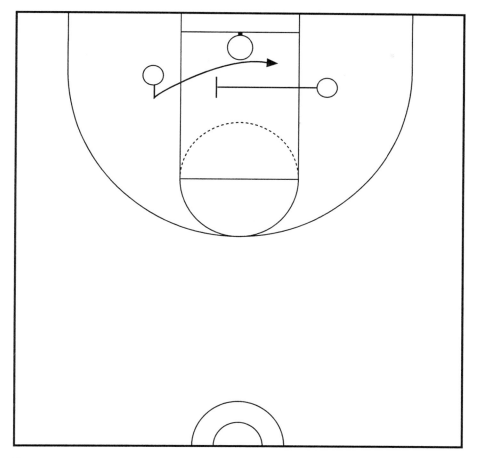

Cross screen

Back Screen

The back screen is used when an offensive player moves away from the basket to set a screen. The cutter breaks either over the top or underneath the screen toward the basket. The back screen is used against defenders who are overplaying.

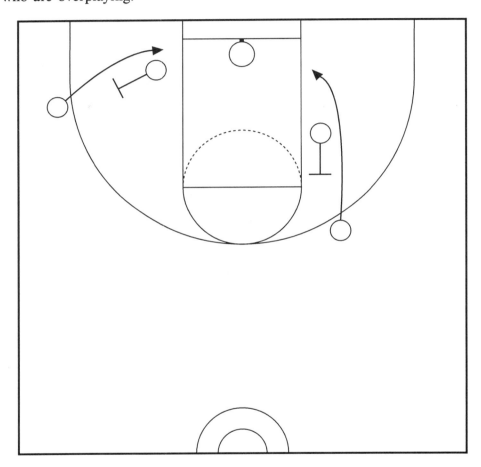

Back screen

Screen on the Ball

The screen on the ball is used to create open shots inside and outside. Screening for the ball handler often creates mismatches in height or speed against teams that switch.

When Setting the Screen:
- Assume a wide stance.
- Roll to the basket by pivoting on the inside foot.
- Swing the arm and shoulder as you roll in order to speed up the turning action.
- Put a target hand in the air.
- Never lose sight of the ball.

Screening on the ball is when an offensive player screens for the ball handler.

When Using the Screen:
- Set up your defender by moving or faking in a direction opposite that of the screen.
- Rub shoulders with the screener as you make your cut.
- Keep your head up and read the defense.

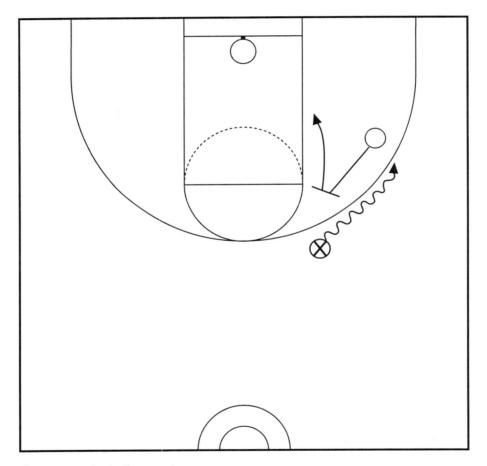

Screen on the ball

Cutting Off the Screen

The purpose of screening is to free teammates from their defenders. To do this, you must cut off the screen at the right time and move to the right place. You must recognize the floor position of your defender in order to make the most productive cut.

Jeff Hornacek, of the Utah Jazz, is excellent at moving without the ball. He knows how to drive his defender into screens and create shooting opportunities. It is very difficult for defenders to stop him from getting open perimeter shots.

Offensive players must become proficient at making the following cuts:

Wing Cut

- Drive your defender into the screen.
- Make a hard cut to the perimeter.

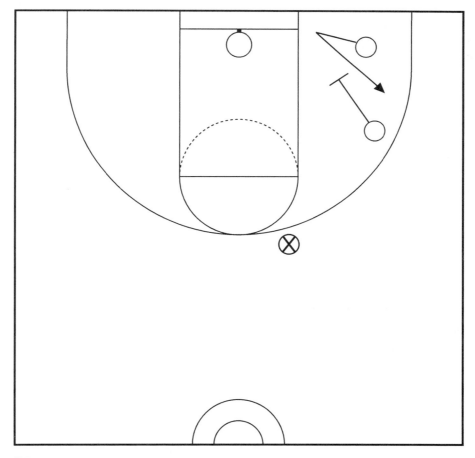

Wing cut

Fade Cut

- Use if your defender sags.
- Cut away from your defender in order to create additional distance from that player.

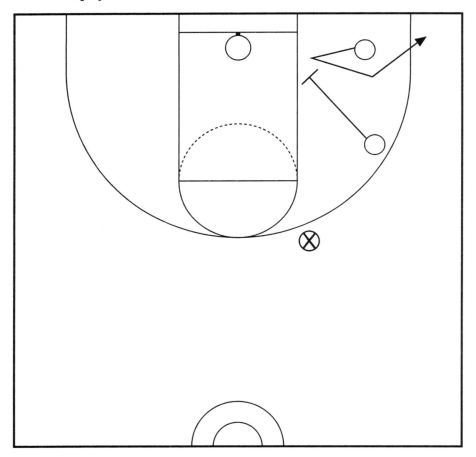

Fade cut

Curl Cut

- Use if your defender is behind and trailing.
- Curl sharply off the screen toward the basket.

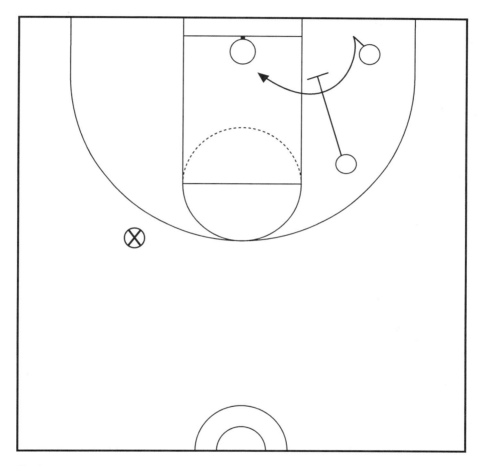

Curl cut

Back Cut

- Use when your defender beats the offensive player over the screen.
- Never lose sight of the ball.
- Push off hard from the floor.
- Present a target for the ball handler.

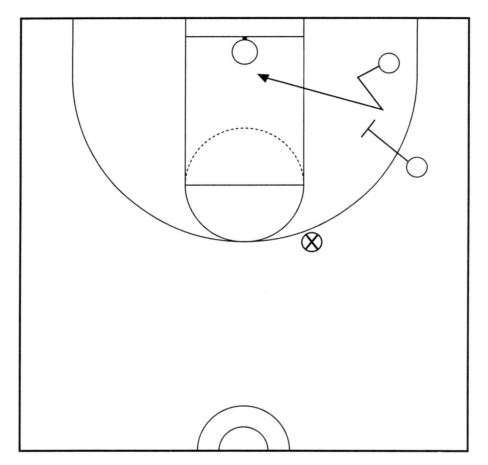

Back cut

10   Offensive Rebounding

Offensive rebounding is a key factor in winning basketball games. Attacking the offensive boards produces high-percentage shots, more free throws, and a distinct psychological advantage.

The 1993 World Champion Chicago Bulls were the best offensive rebounding team in the NBA. Horace Grant and Scottie Pippen provided many second-shot opportunities with their offensive rebounding, and they played a very important role in Chicago's success.

QUALITIES OF OUTSTANDING REBOUNDERS

Successful rebounding depends upon attitude and aggressiveness. Two of the best rebounders in the NBA are Dennis Rodman and Charles Oakley. Although they are not among the tallest players in the league, they demonstrate a rebounding mentality that is unequalled. Rodman averaged more rebounds per game in 1993 than any other NBA player during the past 20 years.

Outstanding rebounders display the following qualities:

Determination
- Rebounding is 75 percent desire and 25 percent ability.
- Make the second effort.
- Do not be blocked out.

Offensive rebounding is a key factor in winning basketball games.

Attitude

- Offensive rebounding is a state of mind.
- Be aggressive.
- Assume that every shot will be missed.

Anticipation

- Know when and where each shot is taken.
- Rebound the help side (70 percent of missed shots are rebounded on the help side).
- Know the rebound characteristics of the ball and rim.
- The timing of your jump is more important than the height.

OFFENSIVE REBOUNDING POSITION

As the shot is taken, you should make every effort to be in position to rebound it if it is missed. Your goal should be to gain the inside position and block out your defender.

If you can't establish the inside position, get even or alongside your defensive player so you have an equal chance for the rebound. Even if you can't get the rebound, always try to get a hand on the ball and keep it alive. By doing this, you may help one of your teammates get the rebound.

Another alternative is to block in the defender who gets too far under the basket. This will neutralize his advantage of the inside position because the rebound will travel over his head.

GUIDELINES FOR OFFENSIVE REBOUNDING

- Do not watch the flight of the ball.
- Start moving toward the offensive boards as soon as the ball leaves the shooter's hands.
- Play every shot as if it were a missed shot.
- Get your hands up in a ready position.
- Do not allow the defensive player to make contact for the block-out.
- Do everything possible to secure the ball or at least make contact with it.

FOOTWORK TO COUNTER THE BLOCK-OUT

You are at a distinct disadvantage when attempting an offensive rebound because the defensive players are closer to the basket. The following techniques will help you gain inside rebounding position:

Crossover Step
- Use when your defender moves too far sideways in an attempt to block out.
- Make a fake in one direction and use a crossover step to move past the defender.
- This can also be combined with false pressure on the defender's back.

Rear Turn and Roll
- Use when your defender has established contact and is in a position between you and the basket.
- Place one foot between your defender's legs and execute a rear pivot.
- Spin off the defender with your hands up.
- Try to establish inside position.

Straight Step
- Use when your defender has not established contact with you.
- Use a long, quick step to get past your defender.

TAKE THE BALL TO THE BASKET

After securing an offensive rebound, take the ball to the basket and finish the play. The following guidelines will help you score after an offensive rebound:

- Land with good body balance.
- Use effective head and shot fakes.
- Make a strong power move toward the basket.
- Concentrate on the basket.
- Protect the ball.
- Use the backboard if possible.
- Be quick without hurrying.

3
Offensive Drills

11   Practicing

Improving your basketball skills requires hours of practice. Many times the difference between becoming a good player and a great player is *how* you practice.

THERE IS NO SUBSTITUTE FOR HARD WORK

There are no shortcuts to success. If you want to be good, you must be willing to work hard. You learn quickly in athletics that achievement is usually in proportion to the price that has been paid. The harder you work, the greater the chance for success.

Basketball skills need to be practiced year-round—there is no off-season for a basketball player. The summer months are the best time for you to work on your individual skills. Identify your weak areas and spend time improving on these fundamentals.

PLAN YOUR PRACTICE TIME WISELY

Using your practice time effectively requires proper planning—deciding in advance what to do, how to do it, and when to do it. Select drills and activities that will help you the most. Write down these drills to develop routines that can be followed easily. It is important to inject variety into your workout sessions so you don't get bored. Do not waste time practicing skills that you will never use in a game. Good planning will enable you to proceed directly toward your goal.

PRACTICE AT GAME SPEED

Going through drills at half speed does not prepare you for live game situations. You must practice as if it were a game. If no one is with you, pretend someone is guarding you. Use your imagination to create game conditions.

REPETITION IS ESSENTIAL

Your execution on game night depends primarily upon conditioned automatic reflex responses. You must practice a skill correctly again and again until it becomes automatic. Endless repetition is the best way to learn a skill so that it becomes a reaction at the instant you need it.

ALWAYS PRACTICE CORRECTLY

For improvement to take place, you must practice the fundamentals correctly. All the drill work in the world means nothing if you perform the skill incorrectly. Remember—"perfect practice makes perfect."

BECOME A STUDENT OF THE GAME

If you really want to improve, study the game of basketball as you would study your favorite subject at school. The following techniques will help you understand the game and become a better player:

- Listen carefully to your coaches.
- Study the techniques of outstanding players.
- Watch videotapes of your play.
- Read instructional books.
- Mentally practice your basketball skills.

To improve, a player should watch videotapes of his play and listen to his coach.

12   Shooting Drills

Players spend the majority of their free time practicing shooting. Unfortunately, most players do not spend this time in a productive manner because they do not simulate game conditions or reinforce the correct shooting techniques. As you practice shooting, remember the following points:
- Take game shots.
- Practice shooting at game speed.
- Simulate game conditions as much as possible.

The following drills, if done regularly, can help you become a better shooter.

INDIVIDUAL SHOOTING DRILLS
Nothing but Net
This drill is an excellent warm-up activity. Start five feet from the basket and attempt to hit nothing but net as you shoot. After making three shots in a row without touching the rim, move to another shooting spot. Use bank shots when shooting from either side. Gradually work your way out to the free-throw line.

Three in a Row
Shoot at one spot and do not move to another spot until you make three shots in a row. Always practice shots that you will use in a game. Practice shooting off the dribble and from a pass to yourself. Add shot fakes prior to shooting.

PARTNER SHOOTING DRILLS

10 Shots

One player is the shooter for 10 consecutive shots; the other player is the rebounder and passer. The shooter moves to various spots on the floor after every shot. Always take game shots and stay within your shooting range. The players exchange positions after 10 shots. As a variation, shoot off the dribble and use shot fakes.

Shoot Until You Miss

One player shoots from a designated spot on the floor; the other player is the rebounder and passer. Continue to shoot until you miss and then exchange positions with the other player.

GROUP SHOOTING DRILLS

Two Ball Shooting

Three players and two balls are needed for this drill. The players set up as a shooter, a passer, and a rebounder. The shooter will move between two designated shooting spots and attempt 10 shots. The rebounder retrieves every shot and throws the ball to the passer. The passer then throws the ball to the shooter. After 10 shots, the players exchange positions. The shooters keep track of the number of made field goals.

Shoot Under Pressure

Three players are needed. A player positioned under the basket begins the drill by throwing a pass to a second player, the shooter. He then rushes at the shooter with his hand up but does not block the shot. The shooter must maintain concentration and shoot over the outstretched hand. The shooter rebounds the shot, passes it to the next shooter, and rushes at him.

SHOOTING GAMES

Beat Michael Jordan

In this drill you are attempting to beat an imaginary Michael Jordan. Begin the game with a free throw. If you make the shot, you receive one point. If you miss the free throw, Jordan gets three points. Now shoot field goals from a designated spot and score one point for yourself if you make the shot and two points for Jordan if you miss. The game is played to 11 points.

Game-Winning Free Throws

Imagine that time has expired in the game and you are shooting a one-and-one free throw. Your team is trailing by one point. You must make two shots to win the game. If you shoot and miss the first attempt, run the length of the court four times. If you make the first shot but miss the second, run the length of the court two times.

"21"

Players take turns shooting a perimeter shot, rebounding, and then shooting a layup. Two points are awarded for a successful perimeter shot and one point for a made layup. The first player to reach 21 is the winner. However, the game must end on a made perimeter shot. After reaching 19 or 20 points, you must make a long shot to complete the scoring.

"33"

Players take turns attempting three-pointers from various spots on the floor. The first player to score 33 points (11 baskets) is the winner.

Free-Throw Game

Each player shoots one free throw at a time. Points are awarded as follows: two points for a made shot that hits only net, one point for a made shot that touches the rim; and minus two points for a missed shot. The first person to get 15 points is the winner.

Around the World

Players shoot from five spots: right corner, right wing, top of the circle, left wing, and left corner. You must make the shot before moving to the next shooting spot. If you miss the shot, you may stay and wait for your next turn, or you can "chance it" and shoot again. However, if you miss the second attempt, you must return back to the shooting spot where you started the game. The winner is the first player to get to the opposite corner and then back to the corner where the game started.

Horse

A player attempts a shot. If the shot is made, then everyone else must make the identical shot. Anyone who misses the shot receives the letter "H." If the first player's shot misses, it is the next player's turn to select the type of shot. Players who get the letters "H," "O," "R," "S," and "E" are eliminated from the game.

Knockout

At least five players are needed for this game. Form a single-file line at a designated shooting spot; the first two players in line have balls. The first player takes a perimeter shot and, if necessary, rebounds the ball and tries to score as quickly as possible. The idea is to make a basket before the player behind you scores, or you are out of the game. If you make the shot, quickly pass the ball back to the next player. The game continues until there is only one player remaining.

Seven-Up

At least four players are needed for this game. Form a single-file line at a designated shooting spot. The first player attempts a perimeter shot. If the shot is made, the second player must make the shot or accumulate one point. If the second player also makes the shot, the third player must hit the shot or is given two points. In other words, whenever you miss a shot, you receive the same number of points as the number of field goals that were made in a row prior to your miss. You are out of the game once you have accumulated seven points. The last player in the game is the winner.

13   Ballhandling Drills

A good basketball player is able to control the ball without losing possession. Games are often lost as a result of careless turnovers. You must strengthen your hands and arms and improve your ballhandling abilities.

Ballhandling includes the offensive skills of passing, catching, and dribbling. The following drills will help you become a better ball handler:

STATIONARY BALLHANDLING DRILLS

Ball Slap

- Hold the ball in one hand and slap it hard with the other.

Tap Drill

- Extend your arms and tap the ball quickly between your fingertips.
- Start the ball over your head, work down toward the floor, and then back up over your head.

Neck Circles

- Move the ball around your neck in a circular motion.

Waist Circles

- Move the ball around your waist as quickly as you can.

Leg Circles

- With your feet shoulder-width apart, move the ball around your right knee.
- Do the same thing around your left knee.
- As a variation, put your feet together and work the ball around your legs.

Figure Eight

- Work the ball in a figure-eight pattern through your legs.

Straddle Flip

- With your feet shoulder-width apart, hold the ball with both hands in front of your legs.
- Drop the ball and bring your hands to the back of your legs and catch the ball before it hits the floor.
- Now drop the ball again and catch it in front; continue this action as quickly as possible.

Pretzel

- With your feet shoulder-width apart, place one hand on the ball in front of your legs and the other hand on the ball behind your legs.
- Drop the ball and reverse the position of your hands.
- Continue this action as quickly as you can.

Ricochet

- Stand straight up with your feet apart.
- Bounce the ball hard between your legs and catch it behind you with both hands.

Run in Place

- Bend over and move your legs in a running pattern, staying in one place.
- Move the ball behind the right leg with the right hand and then behind the left leg with the left hand.
- Continue this action, keeping your feet in a straight line.

STATIONARY DRIBBLING DRILLS

Leg Circles
- With your feet shoulder-width apart, dribble around your right leg using your right hand and left hand.
- Do the same thing dribbling around your left leg.

Figure Eight
- Dribble the ball in a figure-eight pattern through your legs.

Seesaw
- Assume a wide stance with your hands behind your legs.
- Bounce the ball back and forth, always keeping the ball behind your legs.

Draw the Picture
- Stand in one spot and dribble the ball in the following shapes:
- A circle, a square, a cross, and various letters of the alphabet.
- Dribble using your right hand and your left hand.

Front and Back
- Dribble the ball back and forth between your legs using the same hand.
- Do the same thing using the other hand.

Bongo Dribble
- Get on your knees and dribble the ball as fast as you can, alternating hands like you are playing the bongo drums.

Typewriter Dribble
- Get on your knees and dribble using one finger at a time.
- Do the same thing with all fingers, including your thumbs.

Dribble Sit-Ups
- Lay on your back and dribble the ball by your side.
- Maintain control of your dribble as you perform sit-ups.
- Dribble using your right hand and then your left hand.

Wall Dribbling
- Dribble up and down a wall, bouncing the ball as quickly as you can.
- Start as high as you can reach, go down to the floor, and then back up.
- Dribble using your right hand and then your left hand.

360-Degree Dribble
- Use your right foot as the pivot foot and dribble in a circle, making front pivots and reverse pivots.
- Dribble using your right hand and then your left hand.
- Do the same thing using your left foot as the pivot foot.

STATIONARY PASSING DRILLS
Wall Passing
- On the wall make a one-foot square about four feet high to serve as your target (the target should be lowered for the bounce pass).
- Start approximately 12 feet away from the wall.
- Practice the following types of passes: chest, bounce, overhead, baseball, push, and behind-the-back.
- Also practice fakes before passing.

DRIBBLING ON THE MOVE
Figure-Eight Dribble
- As you walk down the floor, dribble the ball in a figure-eight pattern.

Full-Court Dribbling
- Start in the triple-threat position on the baseline.
- Dribble the length of the court using one of the following types of

dribbles: control, speed, change-of-pace, crossover, spin, behind-the-back, or between-the-legs.
- Emphasize certain types of dribbles each workout.
- Make this drill more challenging by imagining there is a defender guarding you.

Suicide Dribble
- Starting on the baseline, dribble with the right hand to the free-throw line, turn, and dribble back to the baseline using the left hand.
- Continue by dribbling to half-court with the right hand and then back to the baseline with the left hand.
- Now dribble to the opposite free-throw line with the right hand, come back with the left, and finish the drill by dribbling to the opposite baseline with the right hand and back again with the left hand.

Stop and Go
- Speed-dribble from the baseline to the free-throw line and stop quickly.
- Maintain your dribble while you are stopped.
- Accelerate with a speed dribble to half-court and stop.
- Accelerate and stop at the free-throw line.
- Finish the drill with a speed dribble to the baseline.
- Do the same thing using your other hand.

Slalom Course
- Place chairs or other obstacles in a straight line approximately 10 feet apart.
- Dribble in and out of the chairs, always using the hand farthest from the obstacle.
- Dribble around the last chair and go through the course again.

Pull-Back, Crossover Drill
- Using the control dribble, advance two dribbles.
- Keep your head up as you retreat two steps using the pull-back dribble.
- Cross the ball over to your other hand and do the same thing.

Dribble-Penetration Drill

- The following dribble moves can be used in this drill: change-of-pace, crossover, inside-out, behind-the-back, and between-the-legs.
- Start at half-court, dribble hard to the foul line, execute a dribble move, and drive to the basket for a score.
- Rebound your shot and advance the ball to half-court, executing a dribble move at the foul line.

STATIONARY TWO-BALL DRIBBLING DRILLS

Control Dribble

- Dribble two balls at the same time.
- Both balls should hit the floor at the same time.
- As a variation, alternate bounces so that one ball is high when the other ball is low.

"X" Drill

- Cross the balls back and forth in front of you.
- As a variation, cross the balls behind your back.

Leg Circles

- Dribble one ball around one leg while you dribble the other ball around the other leg.
- As a variation, dribble two balls in opposite directions around the same leg.

Figure Eight

- Dribble in a figure-eight pattern with both balls going in the same direction.
- As a variation, dribble in a figure-eight pattern with the balls going in opposite directions.

TWO-BALL DRIBBLING DRILLS ON THE MOVE

Straight-Line Dribbling

- Dribble the length of the court, bouncing the balls so they hit the floor at the same time.
- As a variation, dribble the length of the court alternating bounces.

Zig-Zag Dribbling

- Dribble the length of the court, moving from side to side.

14   Inside Drills

Every player must be able to score inside. There are many times during the course of a game when perimeter players can score key baskets in the post area. Versatile offensive scorers develop both their inside and outside games.

The following drills will improve your ability to score inside as well as secure offensive rebounds.

Mikan Drill

The Mikan Drill is designed to improve right- and left-handed hook shots. Start in the middle of the lane, one step from the basket. Take a step, drive the opposite knee up, and shoot a hook shot. Rebound your shot before the ball hits the floor. Take a step and shoot a hook shot on the opposite side. Do not let the ball drop below shoulder level. Continue until you make 15 shots.

Reverse Layups

Start under the basket with your back to the baseline. Take a step, drive the opposite knee up, and shoot a reverse layup. Rebound the shot and shoot a reverse layup on the opposite side. Continue until you make 15 shots.

Tip Drill

Start on either side of the basket, throw the ball against the board, and begin tipping it. Use your fingers and wrist to control the ball; keep your tipping arm fairly straight. At the same time, touch the net with your nontipping hand. Tip the ball eight times and then score. Move to the other side and tip with the opposite hand.

Barkley Drill

This drill helps develop strong hands and explosive inside moves. Start on either side of the basket. Jump up and hit the ball forcefully against the backboard, always maintaining possession of the ball. Land in balance and jump again. Continue for five jumps and then score. Move to the other side of the basket and repeat.

Catch Tips

This drill helps inside players keep the ball high and score quickly. Start on either side of the basket and throw the ball off the board. Rebound with two hands, always keeping the ball above your head. Land in balance and then jump quickly, scoring a basket using a bank shot. Make five baskets and move to the opposite side.

Superman Drill

This drill improves lateral quickness and hand strength. Start outside the free-throw lane, approximately at the block. Throw the ball off the board and retrieve it on the opposite side. Rebound the ball so your feet land outside the free-throw lane. Continue going back and forth across the lane for eight rebounds.

Pick-Ups

This drill requires two players and two balls. It is designed to help inside players develop strong inside moves. Place a ball at each block. The shooter aggressively picks up a ball, makes a power move, and then does the same thing on the opposite side. The second player rebounds the ball and places it on the floor. The players switch positions after the shooter makes eight shots.

Back-to-the-Basket Moves

Start under the basket with your back toward the baseline. Throw the ball out to the edge of the free-throw lane, slightly higher than the block. Go and get the ball and execute an inside move. Rebound the ball and execute the same move on the opposite side. Work on the following moves: drop step, jump hook, turnaround jump shot, wheel to the middle, and up and under.

15 Quickness and Agility Drills

Basketball players are continually starting, stopping, changing directions, and changing speeds. Quickness requires excellent footwork and agility. The following drills will help you in these areas:

ROPE JUMPING

Speed Rope Jumping

Jump as quickly as you can for 60 seconds. Take a 30-second rest and then jump again. Do a total of three sets. Keep track of the number of jumps you make for each set.

Line Rope Jumping

Jump over a line on the floor as you perform your rope jumping. Face the line and jump over it going forward and backward. Record the number of jumps you make in 60 seconds. Now, place your feet parallel to the line. Jump over the line going from side to side for 60 seconds and register the number of jumps you make.

Square Rope Jumping

Jump in the shape of a square as you do your rope jumping. Perform two sets by jumping for 60 seconds and resting for 30 seconds.

Alternate-Feet Rope Jumping

Jump as quickly as you can for 60 seconds by jumping twice on your left foot then twice on your right foot. Perform two sets using a 30-second rest interval.

Three Jumps and a Double Jump

Jump three times and then do a double jump. Do two sets using a 60-second work period and a 30-second rest interval.

FOOT QUICKNESS CIRCUIT

Perform each of the following six drills for 30 seconds. Allow a 15-second rest interval as you move to the next station. Go through the circuit two times.

Slalom

Place tape on the floor in the shape of the letter "V." The width at the top of the "V" should be three to four feet. Start at the base and jump from side to side with your feet together. Always land outside the tape. Jump forward to the top of the "V" and then jump backward to the base of the letter. Always jump with your hands up in a ready position.

"U" Jump

Place tape on the floor in the shape of a cross. Start in the upper right-hand corner. Jump down, across, and up without touching a line. From the upper left-hand corner, jump down, across, and up. (You are jumping in the shape of the letter "U.") Keep your hands up as you jump.

Heel Clicks

Place two parallel strips of tape one to two feet apart. Begin with your right foot outside the right line and your left foot outside the left line. Jump in the air. Click your heels together, and land outside the tape. Keep your hands up and concentrate on quickness and not height as you jump.

Toe Touch

The tape is positioned the same as for the heel clicks; your starting position is also the same. Jump in the air and land inside the lines with your feet next to each other. Quickly jump again so your feet land outside the lines. Keep your hands up and always land inside and outside the lines.

Long Jump

Place a six-foot strip of tape on the floor. Start at the base of the tape and long-jump as far as you can. Use your arms to provide additional power. After landing, shuffle backward to the base of the tape and repeat.

Lateral Jumps

Place a strip of tape on the floor. Jump over the line going from side to side using your right foot. Repeat using your left foot. Do not touch the line and always keep your hands up.

16 Self-Improvement Training Programs

Mastery of the fundamental skills is vital for basketball success. Outstanding players work individually on their basketball maneuvers year-round. They create sound habits through rigorous repetitive work and daily training programs.

This chapter presents sample training programs for both perimeter players and inside players. Every drill listed has been described earlier in the text.

PERIMETER PLAYERS

Workout 1

Quickness/Agility Drills
Speed Rope Jumping
Line Rope Jumping
Square Rope Jumping

Ballhandling Drills
Ball Slap
Tap Drill
Neck Circles
Waist Circles
Leg Circles
Figure Eight

Workout 2

Quickness/Agility Drills
Speed Rope Jumping
Alternate-Feet Rope Jumping
Three Jumps and a Double Jump

Ballhandling Drills
Ball Slap
Figure Eight
Straddle Flip
Pretzel
Ricochet
Run in Place

Stationary Dribbling Drills
  Leg Circles
  Figure Eight
  Front and Back
Dribbling on the Move Drills
  Figure Eight
  Two-Ball Dribbling
  Full-Court Dribbling:
    Control
    Speed
    Change of Pace
Perimeter Shooting Drills
  Nothing but Net
  Three in a Row—off the Dribble
  Beat Michael Jordan
  Three-Point Shooting
One-on-One Moves
  Direct Drive
  Jab Step and Drive
  Shooting after Dribble:
    Spin
    Between the Legs
Free Throws
  Shoot 50 Free Throws

Stationary Dribbling Drills
  Leg Circles
  Figure Eight
  Seesaw
Dribbling on the Move Drills
  Pull-Back, Crossover
  Suicide Dribble
  Full-Court Dribbling:
    Crossover
    Spin
    Behind the Back
    Between the Legs
Perimeter Shooting Drills
  Nothing but Net
  Three in a Row—from a Pass
  Shoot Under Pressure
  Three-Point Shooting
One-on-One Moves
  Crossover Step and Drive
  Rocker Step
  Shooting after Dribble:
    Crossover
    Behind the Back
Free Throws
  Game-Winning Free Throws

INSIDE PLAYERS

Workout 1
Quickness/Agility Drills
  Speed Rope Jumping
  Line Rope Jumping
  Square Rope Jumping

Workout 2
Quickness/Agility Drills
  Speed Rope Jumping
  Alternate-Feet Rope Jumping
  Three Jumps and a Double Jump

Ballhandling Drills
Ball Slap
Tap Drill
Neck Circles
Waist Circles
Leg Circles
Figure Eight
Stationary Dribbling Drills
Leg Circles
Figure Eight
Front and Back
Dribbling on the Move Drills
Full-Court Dribbling:
    Control
    Speed
    Change of Pace
Inside Drills
Mikan Drill
Reverse Layups
Barkley Drill
Tip Drill
Post Moves
Drop Step
Jump Hook
Turnaround Jump Shot
Wheel to the Middle
Up and Under
Perimeter Shooting Drills
Nothing but Net
Spot Shooting (15 feet)
Three in a Row
Free Throws
Shoot 50 Free Throws

Ballhandling Drills
Ball Slap
Figure Eight
Straddle Flip
Pretzel
Ricochet
Run in Place
Stationary Dribbling Drills
Leg Circles
Figure Eight
Seesaw
Dribbling on the Move Drills
Full-Court Dribbling:
    Crossover
    Spin
    Behind the Back
    Between the Legs
Inside Drills
Mikan Drill
Reverse Layups
Catch Tips
Superman Drill
Post Moves
Drop Step
Jump Hook
Turnaround Jump Shot
Wheel to the Middle
Up and Under
Perimeter Shooting Drills
Nothing but Net
Shot Fake, Shoot Off Dribble
Three in a Row
Free Throws
Game-Winning Free Throws

4
Evaluating Basketball Skills

17 Basketball Skills Test

A basketball skills test is a valuable tool to help players recognize their strengths and weaknesses. It identifies specific areas that should be worked on during practice sessions. It will also serve as a measuring device as you chart your improvement.

This basketball performance profile has been prepared with the assistance of Rhonda Fleming, assistant professor of physical education at Limestone College, and Denny Kuiper, former coach at Central Michigan University.

The norms are based on an analysis of the performance of a group of 41 college students ranging in ability from beginners to intercollegiate athletes. The results are divided into the following five categories:

Excellent—90th percentile or higher
Good—70th to 89th percentile
Average—30th to 69th percentile
Below Average—10th to 29th percentile
Poor—9th percentile or lower

TEST ITEMS FOR THE BASKETBALL PERFORMANCE PROFILE

Pressure Shooting

Mark a spot on the floor 15 to 20 feet from the basket. (The distance will vary depending on age and skill level.) Begin the test by attempting a perimeter shot from your designated shooting spot. Rebound the ball and shoot a layup. Dribble back to the shooting spot. Repeat the procedure of shooting a perimeter shot followed by a layup for a total of 60 seconds. Score two points for every successful perimeter shot and one point for every made layup. Calculate your point total.

PRESSURE SHOOTING

	Male	Female
Excellent	25 or better	18 or better
Good	20–24	11–17
Average	12–19	6–10
Below average	9–11	2–5
Poor	8 or less	1 or less

Block Jumps

Stand facing the baseline with your feet together and parallel to the free-throw block. Jump sideways over the block without touching it. Record the number of jumps you make in 30 seconds. Do not count the jump if you land on the free-throw block.

BLOCK JUMPS

	Male	Female
Excellent	89 or better	82 or better
Good	85–88	71–81
Average	71–84	55–70
Below average	65–70	48–54
Poor	64 or less	47 or less

Free Throws

Shoot 25 free throws and record the number of made shots.

FREE THROWS

	Male	Female
Excellent	20 or better	19 or better
Good	18–19	16–18
Average	12–17	7–15
Below average	6–11	4–6
Poor	5 or less	3 or less

Speed Layups

Start on the baseline facing the mid-court line. Speed-dribble to the top of the free-throw circle, turn, and drive to the basket for a layup. Continue for 30 seconds and record the number of successful layups.

SPEED LAYUPS

	Male	Female
Excellent	6 or higher	4 or higher
Good	5	3
Average	3–4	2
Below average	2	1
Poor	1	less than 1

Mikan Drill

Start under the basket and take a short hook shot. Rebound the shot and take a hook shot from the opposite side. Continue alternating sides on every shot. Record the number of shots made in 30 seconds.

MIKAN DRILL

	Male (N–)	Female (N–)
Excellent	18 or better	14 or better
Good	16–17	12–13
Average	11–15	7–11
Below average	7–10	4–6
Poor	6 or less	3 or less

Figure-Eight Ballhandling

Start with your feet shoulder-width apart. Place the ball in one hand between your legs. Move it around one leg in a circular motion. Catch it with your other hand and move it around your other leg in the pattern of a figure eight. Record the number of times you bring the ball to the middle (between your legs) in 30 seconds.

FIGURE-EIGHT BALLHANDLING

	Male	Female
Excellent	66 or better	48 or better
Good	63–65	45–47
Average	49–62	35–44
Below average	40–48	29–34
Poor	39 or less	28 or less

Defensive Slides

Start with your outside foot touching the edge of the free-throw lane. Using the correct defensive slide, move from one side of the lane to the other. Always touch the line with your foot before sliding to the opposite side. Record the number of lines you touch in 30 seconds.

DEFENSIVE SLIDES

	Male	Female
Excellent	25 or better	22 or better
Good	23–24	20–21
Average	19–22	18–19
Below average	16–18	15–17
Poor	15 or less	14 or less

Jump and Reach

Chalk and a wallboard marked off in feet and inches are needed in order to do this test.

Stand sideways next to a wall with the hand farthest from the wall resting comfortably. The other arm is raised vertically with the palm facing the wall and the fingers extended. Place chalk dust on the tips of your fingers. Reach as high as possible with the extended arm and record your reaching height.

Now crouch and jump as high as possible. Record your jumping height.

Your score is determined by subtracting your reaching height from your jumping height. Use the best of three jumps.

JUMP AND REACH

	Male	Female
Excellent	29 or better	19 or better
Good	26–28	17–18
Average	18–25	13–16
Below average	15–17	9–12
Poor	14 or less	8 or less

Wall Pass

For this test you need a flat wall space at least 15 feet long and 7 feet high. In the center of the wall space, draw two vertical parallel lines 3 feet apart. Label these lines A and B. Next, draw a line on the floor parallel to and 8 feet away from the wall. From this line draw two more parallel lines that each meet the wall at a point 18 inches to the outside of the corresponding wall line. Label these lines A and B so that floor line A is closer to wall line B, and vice versa (see accompanying diagram).

Begin the test by standing in Area A. Pass the ball to Area A on the wall and run to Area B so that you can catch the ball on the rebound. Then throw to Area B on the wall and then move back to Area A to receive the pass.

Your score is the number of successful passes made in 30 seconds. You may use any type of pass, but do not count passes that hit in the area *between* wall lines A and B.

WALL PASS

	Male	Female
Excellent	23 or better	17 or better
Good	20–22	15–16
Average	17–19	12–14
Below average	14–16	9–11
Poor	13 or less	8 or less

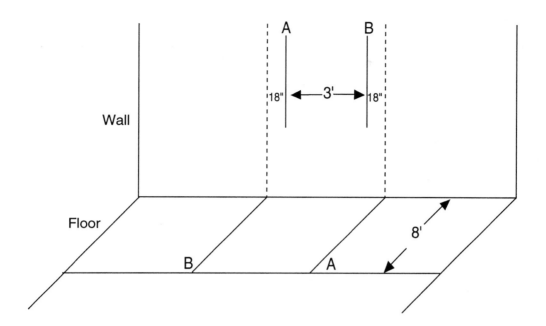

Markings for the Wall-Pass Test

Suicide Dribble

Begin at the baseline facing the mid-court line. Dribble with your right hand out to the free-throw line. Turn and dribble back to the baseline using your left hand. Then dribble to the mid-court line using your right hand, returning to the baseline with your left. Then dribble to the opposite free-throw line with your right hand and finish with a speed dribble back to the baseline with your left hand. Record the number of seconds it takes to complete this course.

SUICIDE DRIBBLE

	Male	Female
Excellent	20 sec. or less	23 sec. or less
Good	20.1–21 sec.	23.1–24.5 sec.
Average	21.1–23 sec.	24.6–28.5 sec.
Below average	23.1–25 sec.	28.6–31 sec.
Poor	25.1 or more sec.	31.1 or more sec.

Appendix

CHECKLIST FOR OFFENSIVE FUNDAMENTALS

This is a summary of the key teaching points for each offensive fundamental. The following checklists can serve as a guide for improving your basketball skills.

Perimeter Shooting
1. Feet are shoulder-width apart.
2. Toes are pointed at the basket.
3. Shooting hand is centered on the ball.
4. Balance hand is positioned on the side of the ball.
5. Ball is cocked in the shooting pocket.
6. Elbow is in front of the wrist and is pointed at the basket.
7. Elbow is kept under the ball.
8. Fingers are thrust up and forward through the ball.
9. Angle of release on the shot is 60 degrees.
10. Head is kept still during the shot.
11. The ball has backspin during the shot.
12. Follow through with complete elbow extension and wrist flexion.

Layup Shot
1. Head is up and eyes are looking at the target.
2. Dribble with the hand away from the defense.

3. Bring the nondribbling hand to the ball and take it up with two hands.
4. Jump off the inside foot and drive the other leg and knee up in the air.
5. Release the ball at the top of the jump.
6. Shoot the ball softly off the top corner of the backboard square.

Free-Throw Shooting Routine

1. Feet are shoulder-width apart with the shooting foot slightly in front.
2. Shooting foot is positioned in line with the basket and turned approximately 10 degrees.
3. Nonshooting foot is turned approximately 45 degrees.
4. Knees are slightly bent.
5. Bounce the ball a set number of times.
6. Shooting hand is centered on the ball.
7. Balance hand is positioned on the side of the ball.
8. Cock the ball in the shooting pocket.
9. Concentrate on the basket
10. Initiate the shot with your legs.
11. Extend the shooting arm in a fluid motion.
12. Follow through.

Passing

1. See the defense and your offensive teammate before passing.
2. Throw the ball to a spot where your teammate can do something with it.
3. Pass the ball away from the defense.
4. Deliver the pass when the receiver is open.
5. Do not wind up when you pass—pass through or past a defender.
6. Keep two hands on the ball until the pass is made.
7. Use fakes to open passing lanes.

Catching

1. Keep your hands above your waist and give a target to the passer.
2. Meet each pass.

3. Keep your eyes on the ball into your hands.
4. Catch the ball with two hands.
5. After receiving a pass, look at your basket and bring the ball into the triple-threat position.

Dribbling
1. Always dribble with a purpose.
2. Keep your head up and see the floor.
3. Dribble with the hand farthest from the defender.
4. Keep the nondribbling arm up for protection.
5. Cup the dribbling hand and spread the fingers comfortably.
6. The dribble is a push-pull motion of the arm, wrist, and fingers.
7. The ball is controlled by the fingers and the pads of the hand.
8. Never pick up your dribble without a pass or a shot.

Starting
1. Lower your shoulder and lean your head in the direction you wish to go.
2. Push hard off your foot.
3. Maintain body lean when starting forward.
4. Use a quick, pumping action of the arms.

Stopping
1. Land with your knees bent.
2. Keep your head up and centered over your body.
3. Maintain a wide base of support.
4. Keep the back fairly straight without bending at the waist.

Pivoting
1. Keep the feet shoulder-width apart and the knees bent.
2. Keep your head up and centered over your body.
3. Pivot by lifting up the heel and turning on the ball of your pivot foot.

Triple-Threat Position

1. Feet are shoulder-width apart and knees are bent.
2. The ball is positioned near the dominant shoulder.
3. Shoulders are facing your basket.
4. Eyes are looking at the basket and seeing the entire floor.
5. From this position, you can quickly do one of three things: shoot, pass, or dribble.

Glossary

air ball—a shot that completely misses the basket and the backboard

assist—a pass that results in an immediate score

backboard—the rounded or rectangular board placed behind the basket

backcourt—that half of the court that is the farthest from the offensive basket; also, the position played by the guards

back-door cut—a cut behind the defender and toward the basket

back screen—a move by an offensive player away from the basket to set a screen for a teammate

ball side—the side of the court on which the ball is located; also called the strong side

bank shot—a shot in which the ball strikes the backboard and then rebounds into the basket

baseball pass—a one-handed pass used to advance the ball to a cutter going toward the basket

baseline—the out-of-bounds line underneath either basket on both ends of the floor

basket—a goal that results in a score; also, the rim through which the ball is thrown

behind-the-back dribble—a dribble behind the body from one hand to the opposite hand

behind-the-back pass—a pass thrown behind the back

between-the-legs dribble—a dribble through the legs from one hand to the opposite hand

block out—establish and maintain a rebounding position between the basket and your opponent

bounce pass—a pass that hits the floor between the passer and the receiver

catch and face—technique for receiving a pass and squaring up to the basket; similar to the triple-threat position

center—often the tallest player on a team; normally plays close to the basket and is responsible for getting rebounds and blocking shots

change-of-pace dribble—alternately slowing down and speeding up in order to penetrate past a defender

chest pass—a two-handed pass thrown from the chest

chin it—the position of the ball after a rebound: directly under the chin with the elbows and fingers up

clear out—when an offensive player leaves an area so the ball handler has more room to maneuver

clock-down cut—a cut toward the baseline by a helpside forward

control dribble—a low dribble used when closely guarded

cross screen—a lateral move by an offensive player to set a screen for a teammate

crossover dribble—a dribble from one hand to the opposite hand in front of the body

crossover step—an offensive move consisting of a jab step followed with a step in the opposite direction

curl cut—a cut off a screen toward the basket; is used when the defender is trailing the cutter

cut—an offensive move to elude a defender or drive to the basket

defense—the act of attempting to prevent your opponent from scoring

down screen—a move by an offensive player toward the baseline to set a screen for a teammate

drive—dribbling toward the basket; also referred to as a dribble drive

dunk—score a basket by driving or stuffing the ball into the basket from above the rim

early offense—the period just after a team has crossed over the midcourt line and set up its half-court offensive

endline—also referred to as the baseline

fade cut—a cut used by an offensive player coming off a screen when the defender is in a sagging position

fake—a technique used to get a defensive player off balance or out of position

fast break—an offensive tactic in which a team rapidly moves the ball the length of the court by means of long passes and/or quick dribble drives in an attempt to score before the opponent can set up its defense

field goal—a basket made while the ball is in play

field goal percentage—the percentage of converted field goal attempts

fish-hook cut—a change-of-direction cut that takes the shape of a fish hook and is used as a pressure release

forwards—two players generally positioned closer to the basket than the guards; they often assume a floor position along the perimeters of the free-throw lane and maneuver both inside and outside

free throw—an unguarded attempt to score from a line 15 feet from the basket

free throw percentage—the percentage of converted free throw attempts

frontcourt—the offensive area of the court from the midcourt line to the baseline; also, the positions played by the forwards and center

front pivot—moving forward while turning on the pivot foot

give and go—an offensive maneuver, sometimes called an inside cut, whereby a player passes to a teammate and cuts for the basket

guards—the two players who typically move the ball from the backcourt into the frontcourt and then position themselves farthest from the basket

help side—the side of the court opposite that of the ball; also called the weak side

high post—an area of the court located near the free-throw line

inside cut—when the offensive player passes the ball to a teammate and cuts to the basket looking for a return pass

jab step—a small step toward the defensive player with the nonpivot foot

jump shot—an offensive shot in which the offensive player's feet leave the floor

jump stop—coming to a full stop by jumping off one foot and landing in a parallel or a staggered stance with both feet hitting the floor at the same time

"L" cut—a cut in the shape of the letter "L" that is used when the defender is in the passing lane but is playing very loosely

layup shot—a close-in shot made when moving to the basket

loading the gun—placing the ball in the shooting pocket with the wrist cocked ready to shoot

low post—an area of the court located near the basket

midcourt line—the line in the middle of the court that separates the frontcourt from the backcourt

offense—the team that has possession of the ball

outlet pass—a pass made from a rebounder to an offensive teammate

overhand layup shot—a layup shot with the shooting hand positioned on the back of the ball with the palm facing the basket

overhead pass—a pass made while the ball is held above the head with both hands

paint—the area inside the free-throw lane

passing lane—the area between two offensive players where a pass could be made

penetration—when the ball is dribbled or passed inside the defensive area toward the basket

pick—a screen set by an offensive player

pivot—the rotation of the body around one foot that is kept in a stationary position

point guard—usually a team's floor leader, who initiates the offense and controls the tempo of the game

post—the area on either side of the free-throw lane

post player—the position usually played by the center

post up—take a position close to, and facing away from, the basket in preparation to receive a pass.

power forward—usually the bigger, stronger forward who plays close to the basket and is responsible for rebounding and inside scoring

power layup shot—a layup used when closely guarded

pull-back dribble—a dribble used to avoid defensive pressure or traps

push pass—used to pass through or past a defender who is guarding closely

rebound—securing the ball off the backboard or the rim after a missed field goal or free-throw attempt

reverse dribble—a dribble move used to change directions; also called a spin dribble

reverse pivot—stepping backward while turning on the pivot foot

rocker step—an offensive move consisting of a jab step followed by a step backward; the player can either shoot or drive, depending on the movement of the defender

screen—an offensive technique used to block or delay an opponent from reaching a desired floor position

screen and roll—when an offensive player screens for the ball handler and then rolls toward the basket

shallow cut—a change-of-direction cut; also called a fish-hook cut

shape up—a term used to describe the movement of the screener toward the ball after the screen has been set

shooting guard—generally, the player who takes the majority of the shots from the perimeter, many of which are three-point attempts

shooting pocket—also referred to as the triple-threat position

small forward—usually bigger than the guards but smaller than the power forward; responsibilities include both inside and outside work

spacing—refers to the positioning of the offensive players, who should be approximately 15 to 18 feet from one another

speed dribble—a high, quick dribble used to advance the ball up the court when there are no defenders blocking your path

spin dribble—a change-of-direction move in which the dribbler's body is always kept between the ball and the defender

stride stop—coming to a full stop by landing on one foot first and then the other foot

three-point shot—a field-goal attempt from outside the three-point line

transition—changing from defense to offense and vice versa

trap—a defensive tactic in which two players double-team the ball handler

triple-threat position—an offensive position from which the ball handler can either shoot, pass, or dribble

turnover—an error or mistake that causes the offensive team to lose possession of the ball

underhand layup shot—a layup shot with the shooting hand in front and under the ball

"V"cut—a fake in one direction and movement in the opposite direction in order to get open for a pass

Index

Driving line, 78–79
Dunk shot, 40

Eagerness, 20
Elbow, 24
Enthusiasm, 9
Ewing, Patrick, 102

Faking, 90
"Figure Eight," 143, 160
Fleming, Rhonda, 157
Floor balance, 106–107
Focus, 5
Follow-through, 28–29, 47
Footwork, 47. *See also* Inside moves
Free throw. *See* Shooting, free throw
"Free Throw Game," 136
Front pivot, 85

Game speed, 132
"Game-Winning Free Throws," 136
Getting open, 96
Goals, 11–12
Grant, Horace, 125
Grip, 22

Hardaway, Tim, 78
Hornacek, Jeff, 121
"HORSE," 137

Inside moves, 93–104
    drills for, 145–47, 152–53
    drop step, 99–100
    jump hook, 101–102
    turnaround jump shot, 102
    up and under, 104
    wheel to the middle, 104

Jab step and drive, 91
Johnson, Kevin, 77
Johnson, Magic, 50
Jordan, Michael, 88, 135
Jump and reach, 161
Jump stop, 84–85

"Knockout," 137
Kuiper, Denny, 157

Layup. *See* Shooting, layup
"Load the Gun," 30

McHale, Kevin, 101
Majerle, Dan, 44
Malone, Karl, 41
Mental toughness, 9, 19
Mikan drill, 145, 160
Mullin, Chris, 105

"Nothing but Net," 30, 134

Oakley, Charles, 125
Offensive skills, 83–87
    checklist for, 165–68
Olajuwon, Hakeem, 104
O'Neal, Shaquille, 99
One-count stop, 47
One-on-one moves, 91–92
Overhand layup, 36

Passing, 50–65
    baseball, 64
    basic elements of, 55, 166
    behind-the-back, 65
    bounce, 61
    and catching, 57–59, 99
    chest, 60
    drills for, 141
    overhead, 62–63
    push, 64
Passing lane, 53–55, 97–98
Paxson, John, 17
Penetration, 77–82
Perimeter moves, 88–92, 151–52
    attacking the defender, 89
    basic principles of, 88
    faking, 90
    one-on-one moves, 91
Perimeter shooting. *See* Shooting,
    perimeter